SOMETHING NEW UNDER THE SUN

SOMETHING NEW UNDER THE SUN

EDUCATION

at

MR. JEFFERSON'S COLLEGE

MEREDITH JUNG-EN WOO

I. VIRTUE

MEREDITH JUNG-EN WOO

BORN IN SEOUL, KOREA, Meredith Jung-En Woo studied at Bowdoin College and received her master's and doctoral degrees in International Affairs, Latin American Studies and Political Science at Columbia University.

The daughter of a Korean diplomat, Woo was a student at a Spanish Catholic high school in Tokyo when she came across a beautiful photograph in *National Geographic* of a house in Maine, shuttered for the winter. Woo brought the photo to one of the nuns teaching at her school to ask where it had been taken. The sister's answer, as well as her mention that Nathaniel Hawthorne had graduated from Bowdoin College, led Woo to complete her undergraduate studies there.

Woo spent the first twelve years of her teaching career at Northwestern University, where she co-founded the Center for International and Comparative Studies. In 2001, Woo joined the faculty at the University of Michigan, where she served as professor of Political Science and Associate Dean for Social Sciences in the College of Literature, Science, and the Arts. Woo came to U.Va. in 2008 to become dean of the College and Graduate School of Arts & Sciences.

Arriving at a time of transition, Woo helped guide the College on a new course. Initiatives in the sciences and global studies, critical faculty hires, and a boom in external research funding have enhanced its national and international stature. During Woo's tenure, the College launched the Institute of the Humanities and Global Cultures, the Quantitative Collaborative, the Asia Institute, and the Joint Institute between the College, Peking University, and Hong Kong University of Science and Technology.

Woo has authored or edited seven books, including *Race to the Swift: State and Finance in Korean Industrialization* and *The Developmental State*, which was translated into Chinese in 2008. Woo also was the executive producer of the award-winning film, *Koryo Saram: The Unreliable People*, a 2006 documentary about Stalin's ethnic cleansing of Koreans living in Far Eastern Russia during the Great Terror.

PREFACE

FROM 2008 TO 2014 I served as dean of the College and Graduate School of Arts and Sciences at the University of Virginia. One of the finest public universities in the nation, it has a fabled provenance, founded in 1819 by Thomas Jefferson, the "Author of America," as Christopher Hitchens called him. The University honors his legacy and hews to his principles, on which it still stands, almost two centuries after its founding. It is perhaps the most American of our universities.

I was an unusual choice to lead the College. Born and

raised in Seoul, and educated at an international school in Tokyo run by Spanish nuns from Madrid, I came to the United States as a foreign student. After receiving my Ph.D. from Columbia, I eventually went on to teach political science at Northwestern University and at the University of Michigan. Along the way I worked closely with international agencies on issues relating to trade and economic development in East Asia. It was only when I turned thirty-three that I became a naturalized American citizen. So when John Casteen, then president of the University, sought me out—he said he wanted above all an outside and dispassionate perspective in this leadership role—I was honored, but also a bit apprehensive.

I was right: In the first week on the job I had dinner in town with an alumnus. He loved the University with a passionate intensity. After scrutinizing me for over two hours, he reminded me yet again that the University of Virginia was created by Thomas Jefferson, and that his intent was to make sure the fledgling republic would actually survive, sustained by an educated citizenry. The College was the heart and soul of it, he said: "That's how important your job is, and don't you forget it!"

This was an injunction that would have been overwhelming for anyone, and especially to a Korean-born dean a few days into her job. But I kept it in my heart, and carried it with me for the next six years. Being the dean of the College has been, like the pursuit of truth, the most joyful burden.

I began writing these essays to translate, as best I could,

the continuing mission of the College for our time and beyond, for our place and beyond. The essays, published first as a blog, also served to bring together the students, faculty, and our far-flung alumni, into conversation. Some of these essays were delivered as speeches—at convocations, move-in days, alumni gatherings—and others are reflections on higher education in Virginia and elsewhere. Regardless of their topic or their venue, they all deal with that indispensible place— the University of Virginia—an institution that has meant so much for our state, our nation and our world.

In this collection, the essays are organized under three headings: virtue, place, and "aristocracy of talent." They appeared as themes in my essay called "Something New Under the Sun," that sought to define my views on the purpose of education at Virginia, and set our course for the future.

The first theme is about the cultivation of virtue—an old fashioned idea, perhaps, but no less urgent and important for being out of fashion. Acquisition of virtue and character lies at the heart of Jeffersonian education philosophy. It is made possible through proper upbringing, the accumulation of knowledge, constancy of practice, and ultimately, habit. Jefferson believed that habituation to virtue was not possible, save through discipline, order, and knowledge. This is an enduring legacy.

The second theme concerns the necessity of acquiring that virtue through a myriad of good relationships. Tal Brewer, one of the philosophers in the College, argued that we cannot fully understand the intrinsic value of any human action without grasping its place and relationship in the overall narrative one wishes to create for oneself: a life well lived. The ability to evaluate human actions—as ipso facto good or bad, and not necessarily useful or gainful—and situate those actions in the full flourishing of life is something that cannot be learned through discursive reasoning. He argued that it can only be learned through example and experience. This speaks to the importance of place: good friendships, teacher-student relationships, and mentorships on "Grounds," together consummate in a genuine intellectual community.

The third theme relates to the gathering the very best talent one can find, from everywhere in the Commonwealth and from anywhere in the world. Thomas Jefferson saw this as an important requirement for his "aristocracy of talent," which he defined as a "naturally occurring" phenomenon among the rich and poor, based on virtue and talent. I have found his expression more compelling and expressive than the currently privileged term of choice, "diversity." The essays under this heading discuss the meaning of this aristocracy, and trace, through a few vignettes, the contour of the eventual inclusion of African-Americans and women within it.

Good relationships, important friendships, and mentors—I have had so many at Virginia. Still, no one taught me more than the students in my seminars, and the students that came to the monthly "coffee with the dean," to discuss their concerns. Many came from immigrant families in northern

11

Virginia: John Al-Haddad with sparkling eyes black as onyx and whose Syrian parents are so proud for their son to be in college; Kyle McGovern who is sharp as a tack, the first generation in his family to attend college; Tahir Ahmad with a large clan back in Pakistan who was curious to consider the pros and cons of arranged marriage; and the beautiful Emma Myers who grew up in Russia and had a fine understanding of the relationship between language and nationalism. They are among the finest examples of the "aristocracy of talent." They have taught me much about the meaning of character, friendship, and honor—and also reminded me why being an educator is one of the most rewarding and important of callings.

I want to thank the friends and faculty who were always there with good counsel, cheer, and support: John Casteen, Teresa Sullivan, Pat Hogan, Pat Lampkin, Karen Van Lengen, Karen Raham, Yoke San Reynolds, Karin Wittenborg, Carol Wood; Tal Brewer, Edith Clowes, Cristina Della Coletta, Ken Elzinga, Francesca Fiorani, Gary Gallagher, Paul Halliday, John Hawley, Craig Huneke, James Hunter, Seunghun Lee, Despina Louca, Mel Leffler, Farzaneh Milani, Jeff Olick, Joe Poon, Joel Rini, Len Schoppa, Judith Shatin, Mike Skrutskie, Lisa Russ Spaar, Gordon Stewart, Michael Suarez, Douglas Taylor, Chris Tilghman, Cindy Wall, Phil Zelikow; Trey Beck, Preston Baldwin, Susan Bram, Lee Caplin, Colby Clark, Allen de Olazarra, Tom Dean, Albert Ernest, David and Suzanne Frisbie, Amy Griffin, Fred Hitz, Neal and Lee Kassell, Richard and Kathy Lee, Blair Labatt, Sandy Miller, Fred Newman,

Sarge Reynolds, Bill Scanlan, Kathy Thornton-Bias, Michael Walsh, Michael Weinstein, Jamie Wilson, and Mary Wolfe. There is a particularly special place in my heart for Barbara Glynn. So many helped me, too many to enumerate.

The College is most unusual and fortunate in having its own set of trustees through the College Foundation Board. The trustees are some of the wisest people I have known, and time and time again I turned to them for advice. They generously gave of their time, their energy, and their heart. The simplest way to thank them all is to single out the leadership of the board over the years: John Nau, Chris Gustafson, Alan Roberts, Jeff Nuechterlein, Locke Ogens, Jay Morse, and Peter Brundage.

I would be remiss in not mentioning two people who joined me early on, and have done so much to place the College on an extraordinary trajectory: Rick Myers who, with great brilliance and a superhuman work ethic, vastly improved the management and finances of the College; and Gene Schutt, who brought his distinguished experience in business to build the endowment for the College, thus ensuring its future.

It is to all of them, and the alumni of the College, that I dedicate this book.

MEREDITH WOO

SOMETHING NEW UNDER THE SUN

ERNEST BOOTS MEAD, who taught Music in the College, once told me about a young man who wrote his final exam on Bach's Goldberg Variations, a beautiful but elusive piece. It consists of thirty movements that explore, through a series of harmonic and rhythmic variations, a theme—but the theme is fleeting and discrete. At the end of the essay the student wrote this postscript: "Mr. Mead, I have experienced many variations in my life. Now, I am in search of a theme."

As the University approaches its bicentennial in 2019, this

is an appropriate time to look back and to look forward; to recall our many "variations" since our founding but also to find our theme: who we are, what shapes our outlook and aspirations, and how we define our mission.

The fundamental fact about the University, and the College that is its core, is that it is a great American institution—American not in the sense of the geographic entity that lies between the shores of two oceans, but in the breathtaking ideals that America represents. It is a university for its students and faculty and an historic place for the nation, part of every American's heritage. But the University is also a cultural institution representing something special—"iconic" seems to be an adjective that the New York Times uses whenever the University is mentioned. As we gather here today to give renewed purpose to this iconic and quintessentially American institution, it is important to trace the influences that have imparted character to this place and charted its path.

Philosophers use the term "habitus" to connote places that are historically situated and derived, a "past that survives in the present," or a "history turned into nature"—our second nature. Habitus is a routine practice or convention, a disposition in a community, influencing the way we make sense of the world around us. This morning I would like to offer three historical narratives that in my view come together to create the "habitus" for the College, and which in turn creates in our students, in the fullness of their innocence, something new and marvelous.

The first narrative has to do with the importance of virtue and character. Among the many wonders of the mind of Thomas Jefferson, one is not often mentioned: his vision for his university remains as vital in the 21st century as it was in the 18th century. Jefferson was already an old man when, with a ruthless singularity of purpose, he dedicated the last nine years of his life to creating his university, vowing to "die in the last ditch" to realize "this immortal boon to our country." In 1818, at the age of 75, Jefferson traveled, on borrowed money, to Rockfish Gap in the Blue Ridge—where he served as chair of a commission and the author of its report. It is in that report, known today as the Rockfish Gap Report, that Jefferson offered the most comprehensive statement of his educational philosophy. Nested at the heart is his desire for the habituation through discipline, order and knowledge, of virtue. Virtue to him was not a "chimera," but something real, to be acquired through upbringing, accumulation of knowledge, constancy of practice, and ultimately, habit.

Professor Tal Brewer, one of our philosophers in the College, argues that we cannot fully understand the intrinsic value of any human action without grasping its place and relationship in the overall narrative one wishes to create for oneself: a life well lived. The ability to evaluate the actions we take as ipso facto good (rather than being driven by desires or utilitarian goals), and to situate it in the full flourishing of life, is something that cannot be learned through discursive reasoning. It can be learned only through example and experience. The importance of the good company of friends, teachers, and mentors is paramount, then, something that Aristotle underscores in his Nicomachean Ethics when he says that "human beings must enter into active intimate relations with each other if they are to understand what sort of being they themselves are, and what aspirations are fitting for them." We remain committed to that ideal of intellectual and ethical community today. That includes being aware and awake to the value of the people around us—and reflecting on the larger meaning of life, including for one that was cut short last spring.

In the Rockfish Gap Report Jefferson also wrote of the need to push the frontiers of knowledge, incessantly and endlessly. He saw knowledge as neither settled nor canonical, but constantly evolving—"indefinite [italics in the original] and to a term which no one can fix or foresee." Fourteen years earlier, then President Jefferson had sent Lewis and Clark across the continent to the "Northwest Territory," to find out what it was that the president had bought from the French with his "Louisiana Purchase." This expedition embodied his idea of evolving, unfixed, indefinite knowledge. Of course it did much more—it doubled the American territory, and revealed that a massive continent stood between the Atlantic and Pacific oceans. Suddenly Jefferson could begin to envision his "empire of liberty," precisely by overturning received wisdom (and sending the cartographers back to the drawing board).

The second narrative is about the importance of

relationship and place. One could not be a person like me, coming from the other side of the globe, and not notice the uncomplicated and pure attachment that people have for the University as a physical place. Perhaps it has to do with the University's early days, when its students were young men from land-holding families—men who inherited the houses they were born in, and for whom honor and virtue were in some sense inseparable from the love of place. But this place was not only home to men of privilege. The love of hearth and home was also felt by African Americans, like Catherine Foster, a seamstress and laundress who built a home and community called Canada which stood in part where the South Lawn is.

Perhaps because I live with my family on the Lawn, this sense of place is always with me. But even if I lived elsewhere, I think the importance of place—our place—cannot be over-emphasized. It is often said that with the digital revolution, higher education gets dislocated and enters cyberspace, the "ether" of our time (like so many for-profit online universities which are publicly traded). But the College is not primarily a dispenser of knowledge—and how can it be, when information and knowledge is becoming perfectly free, a public good? The College is a community where learning is based on a different web, an intricate web of relationships that go beyond digital media. Few of our graduates would trade the experience of four years of being here for a hastier ingestion of what they learned. Make no mistake: we head toward a future where all knowledge can be gathered on the head of a pin—or at least in a thumb drive. But there are still so few who can turn data into information, information into knowledge, and knowledge into wisdom. In this sense the College is a profoundly local place, where students learn to understand the meaning of relationships—in constant interaction with their friends and their professors—which will become the foundation of their quest to forge and nurture their intelligence, to eventually find lives well lived. This love of place, and the habit of anchoring life in a multitude of good relationships, should be portable, travelling with our students wherever they go, to all corners of the world and throughout their lives.

The final narrative relates to the imperative of bringing diverse talents together to solve some of the complex problems facing our society. In 1965 President Lyndon B. Johnson, with one brilliant stroke of his pen, leveled the playing field for immigration and thus changed the demography of this country forevermore. That was the unheralded part of the Civil Rights movement, liberating African-Americans but also terminating invidious racial definitions of who could, and who could not, immigrate to the United States. This opened floodgates that soon brought talents from around the world: a harbinger of a great future imparting unparalleled creativity, energy, and intellectual strength to this country.

This law transformed America's great universities, including Virginia. Within decades of the 1965 immigration law, the children of the new immigrants, no longer bound by legal constraints, became significant and substantial parts of the student body—numerically and intellectually. These new Americans would be dedicated to the motto inscribed on the seal of the United States—e pluribus unum, out of many, one: but unless one understood the pluribus, the unum remained a mystery. And certainly at the core of the pluribus you see today on Grounds, is a respect for scholars, higher education, a special history, and the cultivation of character and virtue, thereby adding deeper hues to the original purposes that founded the University. When I walk down the Lawn and look at the undergraduates in this vibrant place, I realize that the world is not just a vast penumbra that lies beyond the water's edge, but that it is also within the Commonwealth of Virginia, especially in northern Virginia, increasingly a polyglot place with citizens in search of greater opportunities.

In his letter to John Adams in October 1813, Jefferson argued that there is a naturally occurring aristocracy, among the rich and poor, based on virtue and talents—as opposed to the artificial aristocracy founded on wealth and birth. He considered this natural aristocracy as "the most precious gift of nature, for the instruction, the trusts, and the government of society." It is the mission of the College to nurture this natural aristocracy for the university, the state, the nation, and the world. Who knows which of our students will solve the most pressing problems facing us today? It might be a scion of the landed aristocracy like Jefferson, it might be a descendant of Virginia slaves, it might be a young woman from the Punjab or a young man from Nairobi.

These, then, are three narratives that form the theme for the College. The first emphasizes the cultivation of virtue in our students, so that they make decisions not primarily in terms of desires or ambitions but in terms of the larger good, leading toward a life well lived. The second emphasizes the necessity to acquire that virtue through a myriad of good relationships—mentorships and friendships—that the College attracts and provides, a genuine intellectual community. And third, to do all that by being true to our founding ideas, by gathering together the best talents that one can find from everywhere in the Commonwealth and in the world—people who can provide what Scott Page, my friend from Michigan, calls "cognitive diversity."

Let me now turn to our strategy for the future—our goals and objectives—as we try to remain faithful to the themes we lay out for the College.

The retrenchment of the last two years has been a painful experience. But we have learned a great deal from this crisis. We have had to think constantly about where we are and where we want to come out at the end of the process. In the course of these deliberations, we have gained an expert understanding and appreciation of our faculty strengths, in anticipation of the emerging structure and organization of knowledge, fifteen or twenty years down the road. It has also required of us an understanding of the political economy of this country and of the world, and its requirements for manpower at the highest professional levels. As we go through one of the toughest times in the history of the College, when the dust settles we must emerge strengthened and revitalized in our core missions.

First, we must remember that the cultivation of virtue, the expansion of knowledge, and the creation of a natural aristocracy through diversity, can only grow from the rich soil of a community of teachers and students, in a relationship. The strength of the College rests unquestionably on the quality of its undergraduate education, and we must draw the line right there, protect our most precious heritage however we can.

Education for virtue rests on reasoning, not on preaching or recitation of virtues qua virtues. The best way to teach about citizenship is not to extol its virtues but to foster critical thinking, like teaching about citizenship through a close reading of Antigone—an ancient play about a heart-wrenching conflict between the state and the self in time of war. Or we might learn about the complexities of familial relationships through studying King Lear or by watching the Albee play, Who's Afraid of Virginia Woolf. In Chemistry, Professor Brooks Pate—a MacArthur genius fellow—teaches our students about interstellar molecular activity, showing them how vast quantities of data about the galaxy are captured, how they may be sorted into information, then into knowledge, and finally into wisdom about the origins of the universe—and for that matter, about all things. We simply must create more opportunities for seminar and smaller pedagogical settings. It may not be possible to reproduce, in exactly the same shape and manner what Thomas Jefferson said was the best example of the tutor-pupil relationship—that of the "affectionate deportment between father and son." But we also cannot create a space of what the sociologists call anomie in the classroom where the teacher is but a talking head with power-point slides.

Second, we are re-imagining and remapping the structure of knowledge in the College. We are identifying and championing the expertise of our faculty that may have remained hidden in the shadows created by the glare of the disciplines. We will start where it matters, from the foundation, basing ourselves on the strength of the top fifty or so faculty, and figure out how to build on their accomplishments to enhance the strength of the College. Our university grew from the bottom up, and has an enormous fund of experience, heritage, and "habitus" as a result. That will never change. But the ecology of knowledge is too fecund, too complex, and the speed of discovery too fast, to rely on planning from outside. So we need to reverse the process, go from the bottom up, doing what we do best: nurturing local talent, and then building around them. The faculty are the best resource for intuiting and pushing forth the new spirit of the age, both artistic and scientific.

As we remap the intellectual strengths of the College, we also need to make choices about the areas—or subfields—that need to be accentuated and nurtured, as we prune weak or unnecessary branches. No university has every possible department and no department has every possible subfield. We will endeavor to be known for the fields and subfields—some old, some new—in which we have unquestionable strength.

Finally, we need to rethink how to create the best ensemble of all the talents we require to maintain our excellence. We need to call into question the one size fits all model of academic careers. The finest minds in research do not always make the finest teachers. There ought to be enough complexity in the College to attract genius in every sphere, in research, in teaching, in mentoring, and make sure they stay focused on what they do best. The College should welcome all talents—tenure track faculty, researchers, clinicians, artists, designers, professors of practice, alumni with real life experience—all jumping into the heart of knowledge-making.

In a letter to Joseph Priestly in March of 1801, Jefferson spoke with satisfaction about the fruits of the American Revolution. "As the storm is now subsiding, and the horizon becoming serene, it is pleasant to consider the phenomenon with attention. We can no longer say there is nothing new under the sun. For this whole chapter in the history of mankind is new."

Higher education has been transformed in this country through dramatic events: the American Revolution itself, the Civil War, the Depression, the G.I. Bill after World War II, Sputnik, the Civil Rights movement, the arrival of millions of new immigrants to the country, and the digital revolution. We are witness today to another great transformation:

reinvention—under the most demanding constraints of political and economic challenges—of the College that is the core of the University.

How we come out at the end of it in the next couple of years, and the decisions we make, will determine the future of the University and the College—whether we will remain the kind of place that Mr. Jefferson would recognize in all the wisdom and worth of his creation. If we come out of the Great Recession of the last two years only to suffer another body blow, we will unquestionably fall far behind the other great universities. But if we do this right with your support, give meaning and reward to the last two years of cut after cut, and return to great vitality and vibrancy, we will be able to say that in the history of the College and of the American higher education, there is something truly new under the sun.

We will then be able to stay true to our core values of virtue, place and locality, a true educational community of lasting relationships and mutual learning, thus nurturing for ourselves and for the country the gift of Mr. Jefferson's naturally occurring aristocracy.

The Goldberg Variations is a curious piece. Its composition is both intelligible and in the end, ethereal; comprehensible yet utterly original—a little like the nature of inquiry, a little like the College. Just as there is a theme in the College, there is actually a theme in the Goldberg Variations. It is in the opening melody, which, after so many variations, returns at the end to remind us of its original brilliance.

VIRTUE

OUR
HONOR

IN THE LATE fall of 2010 as the economy was beginning to recover from a crisis that destroyed so much of the wealth of the middle class, a number of documentaries and docudramas appeared that asked probing questions about the causes of this catastrophe. One such film was *Inside Job*, about the culpability of the nation's elites—not just on Wall Street and Capitol Hill but at research universities, in faculty offices of "thought leaders" who influence policy. In this film professors appeared as technocrats, publishing papers whose economic analysis benefited the corporations where they served as consultants.

Another 2010 film approached a similar subject from a more celebratory angle. *The Social Network* is about the founding of Facebook in the dormitory rooms of Harvard. Larry Summers, who was then president of Harvard after stepping down as Secretary of the Treasury, is played by an actor who is a dead-ringer for Summers—with the same astute bluntness. Two students, Cameron and Tyler Winklevoss, had arrived in his office to accuse their fellow student, Mark Zuckerberg, of stealing and profiting from their original idea for a social networking site. The Winklevoss twins are handsome, strapping children of privilege, with a clear sense of entitlement, so it is hard to feel sorry for them.

Interesting, however, was the argument the twins advanced: Zuckerberg had violated Harvard's honor code. Cameron Winklevoss recited it for President Summers: "The College expects that all students will be honest and forthcoming in their dealings with members of this community. All students are required to respect public and private ownership. Instances of theft, misappropriation. . . ." Summers interrupts and calls out to his secretary. "Anne?" "Yes sir," she says. "Punch me in the face." Tyler Winklevoss continues quoting from the code: "or unauthorized use will result in disciplinary action, including requirement to withdraw from the College." Summers looks up lazily from his desk, eyes full of exquisite contempt, and says: "and you memorized that instead of doing what?" He tells them that students do not enter into a code of ethics with each other—only with the University, and shoos them out of his office. But all was not lost: the brothers eventually accepted a settlement from Facebook worth a reported $65 million.

The first student-run Honor System in the country was established in 1842 at the University of Virginia. In 1965, Professor Robert Gooch said in an address at Finals that he regarded it as "the finest thing about the University," adding that "the great body of alumni are convinced that their association with the Honor System was the most important, the richest, and the most permanently influential experience which they had during their search for truth as students in this institution." The same could be said today, 170 years after the establishment of our code of honor.

The Honor System at Virginia is renowned not just for its resilience and the reverence with which the students and alumni regard it, but also for the non-negotiable quality of its essence. Administration of the honor system is entirely in the hands of the students, with offenses presented to the Honor Committee, which makes the final decisions, and no appeals are possible—not to the faculty, not to the administration, and not to the Board of Visitors. And year after year, the students affirm the policy of "single sanction": one strike, you are out.

There may be no single explanation for the persistence of these institutional features. It illustrates what social scientists call *path dependency*—perhaps a clumsy way of saying that origins matter, and that once you are set on a course under a complex set of circumstances, it is difficult to veer from that course. The circumstances that set Virginia's honor system off on its original track were violent ones, and hence dead serious.

In Mr. Jefferson's mind the University was the fondest experiment of self-governance—that government is best that governs least. The genius of American institutions, he thought, was incongruent with a disciplinary system that hardens college youth "to disgrace, to corporal punishment, and to servile humiliations." Self- governance, even for advanced teenagers, was the best policy. That proved to be a difficult proposition, however. Many of the first students in Mr. Jefferson's University were from plantation-owning families, young men accustomed to privilege but not always to responsibilities, leading the founder to lament the "vicious irregularities" in habits and disposition among a few of his students.

Some of the irregularities were silly—making shrill noises like "split quill" that penetrated the silent night of the Lawn, tooting away on tin-horns, ringing the college bell, dragging iron-fenders over brick pavements just to hear the racket they made, and exploding fire crackers. (Living on the Lawn, I know whereof he speaks.) But others were, as Mr. Jefferson said, vicious: virtual riots, chanting epithets against European professors, hiding behind masks. Soon the riots became a "tradition," and one unsuspecting professor, who tried to pull the mask off a student, was shot and killed on the spot. Out of this tragedy came a chastened university, and out of this chastening, came the Honor System in 1842.

However it was not until after the Civil War that the Honor System reached its finest hour. The students were from preparatory schools with honor systems, the culture of honorable gentlemen was a shared, living experience, and so the Grounds were simple extensions of hearth and home. As the College grew, there was a fear, reasonable but untested, that it was social homogeneity that made the spirit of honor possible; heterogeneity would render the continuation of the Honor System impossible. Even so the System survived and thrived, yet doubts about its viability persisted—in the 1920s the students were predicting that if enrollment went beyond 2,000 the Honor System would be no more. Today the University enrolls over 20,000 students, ten times more than the presumed breakpoint, with a diversity—in gender, race, class, and culture—of those who genially inhabit the Grounds that would flabbergast even Mr. Jefferson.

Along the way the Honor System has evolved. In 1935 the system adopted (in part to avoid an overload of cases) a simpler code focusing on the pledge not to lie, cheat, or steal. The code survived the challenges of the 1960s that came from many quarters, including the Radical Student Union, which called the Honor System one of the two greatest irrelevancies in the pursuit of knowledge (the other being grading).

The students at the University's Law School were equally disenchanted, with 85 percent of the students interviewed saying that "the spirit of the Honor System at Virginia does not correspond to the ideals and morals of the world outside our doors." Then their report went on to pose this stunning question: "Since there is no honor in the world, why try to force an old outdated concept of integrity on students who are preparing to live in this modern world?" (Anne, punch me in the face.)

No honor in the world? As Prince Hal exits the stage in a scene from Shakespeare's *Henry IV,* the corpulent Falstaff is left to muse on the meaning of honor. "Can honor set a leg? No. Or an arm? No. Or take away the grief of a wound? No. Honor hath no skill in surgery then? No. What is honor? A word. What is that word, honor? Air... Therefore, I will none of it. Honor is a mere scutcheon."

Today few of our institutions are unscathed by misbehavior and scandal: Wall Street, the church, big-time sports, government local and national, the mores of our politicians. Among the two institutions people still hold in high esteem are the military and higher education—two great institutions traditionally cherished for social mobility, and for social and racial integration. Yet only recently we learned of the careless burning of the Koran in Afghanistan, and of the racial hazing that led to the suicide of a Chinese-American solider. Academe grapples with its own sets of problems related to athletics—and at Virginia, we have all been tarnished by a senseless killing in our midst, an event that forces us to examine the terms and boundaries of our cultural norms and behavior. But higher education cannot escape its role in setting moral standards for our society. Honor is not a mere scutcheon—a ceremonial shield—nor is it simply empty air: it is an attribute without which our society cannot function, a principle without which we are left only with broken covenants. Whatever our faults, for two centuries the University of Virginia has pledged itself to the ideal that honor matters, that honor counts.

On many days I walk through the gateway to the University on Hospital Drive. On the arch—we can call it our escutcheon—is a marble slab. Inscribed in marble is this statement: "Enter by this gate way, and seek the way of honor; the light of truth; the will to work for men."

THE MEANING OF AUTHENTIC

WHEN THE STUDENT organizers of the Second-Year Council Dinner Series extended their gracious invitation to me to speak, I asked about the topic. I was surprised that they wanted to hear about me. Suddenly I had a chance at Andy Warhol's dream of fifteen minutes of fame. After a moment of more serious reflection, I realized that the request was a fair one: as their teacher and dean, I ought to be an open book for them to read, one in which they might see a future that means something to them.

But before I turn to my past, let me begin with our present. We have a few more weeks of this brilliant autumn before the deep weeping red of the crape myrtle succumbs to the barren limbs of winter. There will be lots to remember from this October, beginning with the upset victory over twelfth-ranked Georgia Tech. Before the game, I worried that the Yellow Jackets' sting would prove fatal to the Cavaliers. But as time ran out on Georgia Tech, I joined the cheers as a mass of orange and blue poured down the hill, the way that nature loves to fill a vacuum, right past those signs that say "No Spectators Allowed on the Field." The team was engulfed by ecstatic students singing the Good Old Song.

That will be a fond recollection of October 2011. But this is also the month that began with the passing of Steven Jobs. I was riveted by all the commentaries and eulogies—not because I am a Jobs fan: I am not. I resent him for his iPods that intruded into the space and time I might otherwise have had with my children; and for his iPhones that have prevented any possibility of solitude from work; like so many of us, the first thing I do in the morning and the last thing I do at night is read and write e-mail in bed.

New York Times columnist David Brooks used the passing of Jobs to underscore the worrisome slowdown in innovation in America. He cited Tyler Cowen's recent book *The Great Stagnation*, Neal Stephenson's essay "Innovation Starvation," and Peter Thiel's "The End of the Future." For Brooks, Jobs' death seemed to mark the end of hope. It does not, but I understand why he thinks the Promethean moment has passed. You second-year students, who had not even been born in the 1980s, cannot remember the very same fears of American decline and Japanese advance that dominated that decade. People in Detroit decided that they better start learning Japanese. They didn't realize that the center of world innovation had not in fact crossed the Pacific. It was just three time zones away, in Palo Alto. Three decades later, America remains the world's leader in high technology.

In other words, the fire of Prometheus only fades for a moment before it is lit again. And no matter how many thousands of universities are built in China and India, I will always bet that that flame will be kindled in this country, at a university like ours, a university that Mr. Jefferson founded on a model that, when all is said and done, hasn't changed much over two centuries—it's a brilliant flame that keeps on burning brightly.

Still, it must be said that Steve Jobs personified a great era in modern American history, the fortuitous synchronicity of cultures and sensibilities that were both original and time bound. It is always wonderful to be young and talented, but to be so in the penumbra of the 1960s cultural revolutions was quite special. Here comes a baby with a curious provenance (Syrian father, German-American mother, adopted by a machinist's family with no college degrees), who dabbled in tie-died shirts, LSD, ashrams in India, and communes in Oregon. Steve Jobs became what he became by imbibing and personifying the spirit of the age, and then, through the force of his personality and his formidable talents, he transcended it.

He and Steve Wozniak began with a little personal computer in 1976, then the foundational Apple II in 1978, then the Mac, then all the i-this, i-that and i-other. There will be another Jobs, to be sure, and I hope he/she is sitting here in this room. That will be a person who comes out of the zeitgeist, the spirit of the age, takes full advantage of it, runs with it, and makes from this present a future that none of us could imagine.

Where does that leave me? When I was your age, I felt like I had just stepped off a spaceship, flying from my home planet of Seoul, Korea to a planet called Brunswick, Maine, with its Bowdoin College. I did not understand the country I landed in, let alone understand the zeitgeist, how it came to be, where it was going. I was an alien in a country where for people my age, popularity seemed more important than anything. When I wasn't invited to join one of the ten fraternity houses on campus then, I spent most of my time in college shooting pool in the student union—or with the friends I found at the Afro-Am Center, listening to Marvin Gaye and Jimi Hendrix. I didn't really know who they were; I just knew they were cool.

America is an idiosyncratic country, a difficult country to understand if you weren't born here—or perhaps even if you were. The founding documents of this country say that certain truths are "self-evident," and I felt like a fool for not understanding what they are. But Americans can also be provincial, not grasping that these same truths are decidedly not self-evident in many cultures around the world.

I came from a country that went from very poor to very rich in my lifetime. It is a country that honors its scholarly tradition. I come from a sprawling clan, so many uncles and aunts that I never knew existed, and yet among all those cousins, I can't think of anyone who didn't go to college. I knew them all well, because they all showed up at our house in Seoul to be fed and housed when they came to college in the capital.

The country I grew up in was the antithesis of what we hold dear in this country. It wasn't democratic; it was a dictatorship. Freedom was regulated rather than celebrated, night and day was separated by curfews—the sirens at midnight, and the dropping of morning newspapers in the dark courtyard shortly after the lifting of the curfew at 4 a.m. Why the curfew? Allegedly, to look for communists, but in fact to cow the population. Yet despite the absence of civil liberties, there was still a spirit of enrichment, hope, and a promise of their place in the sun. Koreans are a people who believe in their bones that theirs is one of the finest civilizations in the world, and that they could be great again if they could just make it through the twentieth century.

My father was an economic planner in a country where economic planning meant something, designing five-year plans for the industries that they wanted to encourage, with micro-economic planning to make it happen. He would leave home at 5 a.m. to visit the local market, for a spot check on the

41

price of charcoal briquettes (used to heat most homes) and of squares of tofu. This would tell him how prices were fluctuating throughout the country. In fifty years, civil servants like my father took a country poor by every measure except education, set progressive goals and export targets—which were met year after year after year and which transcended anything in modern times to that point: double-digit growth in GNP from 1965 to 1997. (China has taken the same model and surpassed everyone.)

I remember the hardships. I remember showing up in school at 6:30 a.m. to sweep the streets with my classmates. Korea is a cold country and in the winter my fingers froze to the broomstick. In gym class, we learned to throw plastic grenades in case we had to throw real ones at North Korean soldiers.

I lived in Korea until I was fourteen; then I finished high school in Tokyo. No matter how harsh the environment we grow up in, it is still *your* childhood, it is who you are, it is the meaning of the authentic. I look back on my youth as a period of unprecedented hope and eventual accomplishment.

I have in my heart a complicated understanding about cultures and cultural authenticity that defies all principles and rules, that defies all the voices that tell you what you *can't* do (and they were all over Korea in the 1960s). Steve Jobs, you and I are all creatures of the surroundings that we inhabit and make authentic; and it is when you are authentic—because you have imbibed the spirit of the age and its possibilities and hopes—that all the obstacles and differences melt away, and we seek what is genuine and confident and true.

Throughout my studies at Bowdoin and later at Columbia, I never thought of myself as part of the "mainstream." But it never bothered me that I was on the outside looking in. By training and temperament I am a scholar—and by definition, a scholar is not a participant in the events as they occur—they are observers. There is a little-noticed advantage in not being in the mainstream—standing there, your nose pressed against the window, on the outside looking in. From that vantage point you can observe many things that active participants and mainstreamers do not see.

Eric Hobsbawm, in his autobiography, *A Twentieth Century Life*, spoke of the contributions that the Jewish people have made to the modern world, a contribution so disproportionate to their numbers. Part of the genius that they brought to Europe and later to the United States was that they were outsiders—essential outsiders—seeing things that insiders often cannot. Over the course of American history, outsiders have brought so much talent to this country.

But outsiders don't see and hear everything. I have to admit that thirty years later I am still deaf to the genius of Jimi Hendrix. Still, there are other aspects of American life that I have lived, imbibed, and thoroughly understood, to the point that they are in my DNA—things that have allowed me to continue to be authentic to myself as I was as a ten-year-old child, and to myself today, as teacher and dean to you. However, I don't think I became an American on university campuses, reading philosophy and literature in a second language. I did so sitting in the bleachers at Little League games. My son was a first-baseman. Even though he was neither tall nor left-handed, as first-basemen are supposed to be, he was an excellent fielder. The trophy he won read, "If he can touch it, he can catch it." I watched my son—an American son, or a son becoming American—in his "Arts' Yankees" uniform, and little by little, as if through osmosis, I came to feel that I belonged, too. It is another kind of authenticity.

Early in 2008 someone called to ask if I might consider the position of dean of Arts & Sciences at the University of Virginia. Virginia! I thought it was the most exotic word I'd ever heard in my life—but it also rang true. I remember coming to interview here in late February 2008, sitting in the back garden of one of the pavilions, and watching purple pansies in full bloom. There was sweetness in the air, sunlight spread through the garden: it was glorious, but it was just a beginning. Now that I am part of it, I have nothing but good will, high hopes, and such great good fortune to be part of a university with students like you—and that takes such great pains to remain authentic to its original meaning and purpose.

LEADERSHIP
AT MIDLIFE

THE ORIENTATION FOR department chairs and program directors is the last event of the summer, and the first event of the academic year, the cockcrow heralding a new day, a new season, a new year. So at this time I always find myself excited, and full of hope.

I have good reason to feel excited, and not just because a new beginning is always exciting—but because of the caliber of the academic leadership you represent. All of you have been appointed or reappointed within the last three years, to work seamlessly with your faculty and with the dean's office.

I doff my cap to those of you who have been stewarding your departments and programs with such rare good cheer, wisdom and frugality. There is no question that the last three years were extraordinary for public institutions, demanding patience, fortitude and creativity. For those of you about to begin your duties as chair, you have invaluable resources in your more experienced colleagues. I hope the next three years will be a rewarding and enlightening period in your professional career.

There is something unusual about the academic leadership that you have assumed. One measure of that unusualness is that so little has been written about it—except perhaps in David Lodge's satires. A large portion of airport bookstore revenue derives from books on management and leadership, of everything from how to be a Boy Scout leader to running a pet shop to leading a global Fortune 500 company. But university leadership below the presidential level is seemingly an esoteric art, important to those belonging to an academic guild, but with little relevance for the "real world."

Most of us weren't born or trained as leaders; instead, leadership is often thrust upon us—and at midlife, after we have moved up to the rank of full professor. I was in my mid-forties when I was appointed a center director—a job with no manual; the training was on-the-job. I had never really collaborated with a team, preferring the freedom and autonomy of single-author scholarship. Feeling inadequate,

I wondered if "academic leadership" was not an oxymoron.

I wasn't the only one to ponder that issue. In "Science as a Vocation," Max Weber dwelt at length on the inadequacy of scholars and teachers as leaders. Football coaches are leaders, he said, but the qualities that make a man an excellent scholar and academic teacher are not the qualities that make him a leader; if a teacher proves to be a good leader, it is purely accidental.

Regardless of that Teutonic disparagement, the reality is that American universities are not corporate hierarchies. Rather, the leadership you are called upon to exercise is a collegial one—you are a leader in the sense of primus inter pares. This requires both thought and creativity—if not a redefinition of what it means to be a leader. We all know how hard it is to get people to do what they ought to do, without being asked or told. It is harder when the incentives for non-cooperation are stacked against administrators. Of the triad we expect of the faculty—teaching, service and scholarship—it is often the last that is more intellectually compelling and rewarding.

This managerial relationship, combined with a culture that is inherent to academic settings of inquisitiveness and openness, requires that chairs navigate relationships horizontally and not vertically. In many ways, however, that makes "academic leadership" less an oxymoron than a harbinger of the future in workplace organization. Collegial leadership is the modal form of leadership in a democracy, here and in our relationship with the world—even if the current Congress missed that memo. It is leadership through persuasion and example, not by hierarchy or threat.

The best skills of your collegial leadership are in demand as never before. The decade ahead will see the College grow and be transformed in ways rarely seen before. As you know, the College anticipates absorbing the majority of the undergraduate enrollment planned by the University through 2018-2019, and with it, there will be a corresponding growth in faculty size; we estimate it will produce 63 new faculty lines. Add to that the reality of the retirement surge of eminent faculty, especially in the sciences, and the normal turnover associated with departures, and we anticipate mounting more than 200 faculty searches in the next five to seven years. To give you some sense of this magnitude, this is over one third of the total tenured and tenure-track faculty in the College and Graduate School of Arts & Sciences.

There are stupendous challenges ahead of us, not the least of which is the sharp erosion in the competitiveness of our salary structure, as the University enters its fourth year of no salary increase for faculty and staff. The static compensation issue is very much at the forefront of our thinking at the moment, because it is absolutely critical for recruiting and maintaining excellent faculty as well as their morale. On top of this, we must also initiate a program to create more faculty positions over and beyond the 63 mentioned above, in order to bring down the ratio of students per faculty. The success of this program—a new campaign we expect to launch for the College in the fall—would mean that the total number of searches for the next seven years could be as high as 265.

A year ago, I delivered a vision statement for the College entitled "Something New Under the Sun," which was a paraphrase of Mr. Jefferson, who was in turn paraphrasing Ecclesiastes to describe the utter uniqueness of the American Republic. In the coming decade we have an opportunity, through faculty turnover and expansion, curriculum reform and new scholarly research, to reinvent the College and create something truly new under the sun in American higher education.

This new reality dictates that the most important role of chairs is to recruit top scholars and promote excellence. This often means being hard-nosed in maintaining high standards, but it also means being creative in finding diamonds in the rough, budding scholars whose promising futures lie ahead. Facing such a large turnover in the next decade, the importance of your role, and your firm guiding hands, is immense.

49

Max Weber, who was so (self-) critical of scholars as leaders, had also written a companion and better-known piece called "Politics as a Vocation." In that essay he argued that the three eminent qualities in political leadership are passion, a feeling of responsibility, and a sense of proportion. By passion he meant the devotion to a cause—to take a stance—ira et studium. By responsibility he meant a "romanticism of the intellectually interesting," rather than the easy path of routine bureaucratic duty. And by a sense of proportion, he meant an ability to remain realistic and dispassionate, to retain a sense of distance while getting things done. The forging of passion and dispassion in the soul of the modern politician was the vexing question that he sought to understand. Had he lived another hundred years, however, he would have seen that the question is no less germane for the academic leaders of the twenty-first century.

In 1911 Weber wrote that German students hated intellectualism as the worst devil. Not despairing, Weber exhorted them to greater effort: "Mind you, the devil is old; grow old to understand him." Most of us were in midlife before embarking on our path of academic leadership, and that is a strength; we are fortunate to have gotten old enough to know a little of the devil in life. Watching years come and go, having experience, learning from our own and others' mistakes, makes us better leaders. It helps us regard life with a certain dispassion, having known the twists and turns, understanding the possibilities and limits. It is another way of saying that the Owl of Minerva flies at dusk—or in our case, let us hope, at mid-career.

WHAT DO WOMEN WANT?

I AM HUMBLED to have been selected this year for the Elizabeth Zintl Leadership Award, presented by the Women's Center. I have long admired the work of the Women's Center.

The Center is an indispensable organization. It has remained true to the originating and essential purpose of the University—the education and generation of a democratic citizenry—while evolving over time to incorporate the changing Zeitgeist, reaching out to increasingly diverse and heterogeneous constituencies. In so doing it has always maintained its bias for the vulnerable—young women or young men, of different racial and ethnic groups, and sexual orientations—trying to bring to reality a goal that is often aspired to but rarely obtained: a truly inclusive community. Sharon Davie's leadership has been inspiring, especially in the astute way in which she understands and articulates the stresses of our society, and empowers our students to withstand and overcome difficulties that result from those stresses.

I am also honored to be joining the distinguished ranks of women leaders who have won this award in the past. One cannot celebrate the significant role of women leaders at the University of Virginia without mentioning Teresa Sullivan, our President, and the first woman in history to be bestowed with this honor. I am particularly grateful for President Sullivan's unwavering commitment to our University and to the example of grace and fortitude she sets for all women, both here in Charlottesville and around the world.

Reflecting on the leadership of President Sullivan and other women at all levels, and throughout its history at the University, I cannot help but think that they exemplify a different kind of woman than that typically portrayed, and under discussion, in our society.

The timing of this award coincides with a national debate on women's leadership, amid much handwringing about whether "women can have it all." In the space of the past year, women of extraordinary accomplishments have come forward to debate this question, and to offer perspectives from their experience, of being women, mothers, professionals, and leaders.

Sheryl Sandberg, the chief operating officer of Facebook, is a woman who has it all. In a book called *Lean In*, she issued a clarion call for women to fight discrimination in the work place, by the means of the elbow—both greased and sharp—to attain leadership positions. (Since it came out the book has sold a million copies and topped the New York Times bestseller list: as Billie Holiday sings in "God Bless the Child," "Them that's got shall get.")

A woman no less accomplished has also chimed in. In an article in the Atlantic, titled "Why Women Still Can't Have It All," Anne-Marie Slaughter—former dean of Princeton's Woodrow Wilson School and former Director of Policy Planning at the State Department—chronicled the impossibility of "having it all." She arrived at a point where no woman had ever been, in a post that George F. Kennan once held; from that perch she was able to hold forth on and influence issues of signal importance—from the wars and democratic prospects in the Middle East, to international human rights, youth in China, and gender equality here and everywhere. In the end, it was too much for one woman to handle. The straw that broke the camel's back was her teenage son, who was acting up as teenagers often do, demanding her attention.

Then comes another well-publicized confessional, this week from Debora Spar, the president of Barnard College. In "Wonder Women: Sex, Power, and the Quest for Perfection," she suggests a compromise, the advice that perfection is a fool's errand, and satisfaction can be found in prioritizing women's various commitments.

This debate on "having it all," coming as it does after the feminist revolution seeking equal rights for women, strikes me as curiously self-absorbed. It is a debate that is largely irrelevant for most of humanity, women or men. It is a back-and-forth conversation among professionals who have reached a stratospheric level of accomplishment. Few working women are worth over $1 billion as Sheryl Sandberg is said to be; few have straddled the heights of the policy-making world and academic administration as has Anne-Marie Slaughter; only a few women lead an elite liberal arts institution like Barnard.

But this is a conversation that has drawn great national attention, and has piqued the curiosity of our undergraduate women. In bewilderment, they have asked me: "What does it mean, we can't have it all?" This flies in the face of all their youthful accomplishments and aspirations. They have asked for conversations, which I hold in my pavilion living room, and we will continue these discussions this fall.

I am not quite sure how to understand this debate about "having it all," except as a reflection of what the Canadian philosopher C. B. Macpherson once called "possessive individualism," in which an individual is conceived as a proprietor of her skills and talent, acquired and traded on the open market; the more success, the more thirst for acquisition and consumption. He traced this conception of the individual through Hobbes, Harrington, and Locke, and argued that it permeated our liberal society. Such a conception, he thought, thwarts us in obtaining our full potential as rational and moral beings, and blocks us in friendship and love, which is premised in giving and sharing, not in the acquisition of advantages.

Let me take a moment to discuss women at this university who do not fit that stereotype, but instead give and share. Pamela Joseph is the research administrator in our Physics Department. For over thirty years she helped prepare proposals for external funding, going carefully over every number, every column, every punctuation mark in every proposal, so that the rewards can go to the scientists she supports. She is a woman at work, and every bit a leader without whom funding for Physics would gravely suffer. She has been doing this for 33 years.

Last month Debbie Best, one of the finest staff members in the College of Arts and Sciences and currently the administrative assistant at the Carter Woodson Institute, lost her 27 year-old daughter, Nicole. Nicole was a correctional officer with the state, she was exhausted after work, and her car went off I-64 near Palmyra. Amid the worst catastrophe that could befall her, Debbie was back at work to help the undergraduates at Carter Woodson—now streaming back to school and needing her attention and guidance.

I think of women, too, who have preceded me in winning the Zintl Award—women at work, whose accomplishments are measured by the durable communities that they have created at the University. Karin Wittenborg, one of the leading university librarians in the nation, has created in the libraries a magical space like none I know. Alderman and the other libraries that she supervises are beautiful, safe, free spaces. The libraries are repositories of knowledge. Thomas Jefferson famously said that knowledge is power, knowledge is safety, and knowledge is happiness. Surveying the students in Alderman, with their food, drinks, gadgets and backpacks, I can't help but thinking that she has made the Jeffersonian dictum come to life, and especially to the last point about happiness. And she has made the scholars in the University feel like grand pashas, by delivering directly to their offices the books and documents which she lets them keep, for as long as they want and need them.

56

I would be remiss in not mentioning another past awardee, Pat Lampkin, our vice president for student affairs. I have often said, and will say it again, that she is the Atlas on whose shoulders rests the burden of the safety of our students. She knows more about them than even the vaunted and very intrusive National Security Agency. She is on call twenty-four-seven, knowing in her bones that the safety she provides—emotional and physical—is the space in which they can grow and thrive, as scholars and athletes and sons and daughters: and as human beings.

Sigmund Freud once famously asked, "What does a woman want?" It was the greatest question that has never been answered, he said, and one he was not "able to answer despite [his] thirty years of research into the feminine soul." Let me furnish an answer by a woman, Hannah Arendt. A woman, like a man, is homo faber—one who does, one who shapes, one who works. She is not a women laboring on someone else's behalf, but a woman at work. With her skills, knowledge, tools and passions, she fabricates a social world that is distinct from anything given in nature. She is a builder of things, of edifices, of communities, to demarcate a "common world" of spaces and institutions within which a shared life unfolds, thrives, and finds its own rewards.

The women at Virginia are the architects of their destiny: skilled, accomplished, and compassionate. They are, as is written in the Women's Center mission statement, "shapers of the world"—women having an impact beyond the personal sphere. The best of them never cared much to "have it all." Instead they have given their all for the community that I am so proud to call mine—and ours.

57

HENRY ADAMS: FELLOW VIRGINIAN

58

ON BEHALF OF the College of Arts & Sciences, its faculty and staff, let me welcome you, on this glorious and cloudless day, to our extended family. We have gathered in Cabell Hall today to participate in a tradition that began nearly two centuries ago: to offer the finest education to our students. Two thirds of you are from the Commonwealth of Virginia. One third of you come from others states and nations. Regardless of your origin, beginning today, you will always be Virginians. And so I begin my remarks by reflecting on the life of a fellow Virginian: Henry Adams.

Henry Adams was one of the greatest historians this country has produced. He was the American Gibbon, who witnessed and chronicled not the decline and fall of an empire but the rise of a great civilization. His grandfather was John Quincy Adams, the sixth President, and his great grandfather, John Adams, the second President, both from Massachusetts. He was something of a rebel in his own family and took a dim view of the achievements of the elder Adamses. For Henry Adams, America's greatest presidents were Virginians—especially Washington and Jefferson, whom he considered paradigms of what is best in our national character and its aspiration.

In his study of Henry Adams, author Garry Wills argues that by temperament and choice, Henry Adams was a Virginian; and that his emotional and ideological compass pointed south since he was a child. At Harvard—where, Adams said, the Unitarian clergy produced in its students a mind "on which only a water-mark had been stamped"—his favorite fellow students were Virginians, although there were only three. One of them was a son of Robert E. Lee.

In his autobiography, The Education of Henry Adams, Adams says that he recognized in the younger Lee a kindred spirit—an anachronism, just as he thought he was—an untimely man: Lee was a quintessential Virginian of the eighteenth century, he wrote, much as Adams was a Bostonian of the same age. And Adams delighted in Lee because everything he represented was the obverse of the Puritan Adams family—warm, accepting, genteel, tainted but forgiving. He admired in particular Lee's "liberal openness toward all he liked," and his "Virginian habit of command," taking "leadership as his natural habit." Virginians could be indulgent, and he went to some lengths describing their vices, but his affection remained unbroken and warm.

Henry Adams' conception of himself as a walking anachronism formed the basis of his brooding autobiography. His life spanned much of the nineteenth century, but his education, based on the classics, was quintessentially eighteenth. Reflecting on his education at the turn of the twentieth century, the American Gibbon felt that as an historian he had little to teach his students because he could not comprehend the spirit of the new age. Science and technology would require a different kind of mind, he thought.

It was in Chicago that Adams expressed the full measure of his bewilderment at the American engine of progress. Walking among the wonders of the 1893 Columbian Exposition, he decided that even Harvard dons would be reduced to the level of "retarded minds" trying to fathom "a watt or an ampere or an erg" (just as many are today with terabytes and nanobots). Barely was the Columbian Exposition a memory before X-rays came along, and then radium and atoms—"absolute, supersensual, occult" discoveries. By 1904 Adams had himself become "a howling, steaming, exploding, Marconing, radiumating, automobiling maniac."

A man of the twentieth century, Adams wrote, would "think in complexities unimaginable to an earlier mind. To him, the nineteenth century would stand on the same plane with the fourth—equally childlike—and he would only wonder how both of them, knowing so little and so weak in force, should have done so much. Perhaps he might go back, in 1764, to sit with Gibbon on the steps of Ara Coeli."

I understand that fear. Adams heard the roar of the rushing waterfall at the turn of the last century. I hear it today, coming even faster, bringing with it a similar fear, terror, and exhilaration at the speed of new knowledge. In what complexities will the Class of 2014 think? We don't know, but we do know they will be twenty-first century men and women, people for whom (quite unlike us) the twentieth century is of the past.

Meanwhile our College is showing them the way. In the Chemistry department we make fundamental molecular-level discoveries to help the world change rapidly from a petroleum-based energy model to an accessible system based on a combination of natural gas, wind, biomass, nuclear and solar energies.

Our biologists are leading a major shift, studying life as an integrated network spanning multiple levels of biological organization. Formerly disparate disciplines are becoming more interconnected by discerning a common set of theoretical principles. Collaborations are already occurring in structural biology, proteomics, and combinatorial chemistry.

High performance computing, complex theory, and statistics will increasingly form the conceptual basis for exploring the universe of new data.

Our psychologists work in and with sixteen departments and units to build on their strengths in electroencephalography and fMRI to study human behavior from childhood to dotage, from cradle to grave; and in Astronomy, Astrophysics and Astrochemistry, our scientists are at the forefront of understanding the interstellar chemical processes that produce the molecules that form planets and may be responsible for seeding the universe with the chemical components that produce life.

In the College we endeavor to give our students, whether they study the sciences or not, the scientific vocabulary for the new century, the language they need to develop the kind of contemporary mind—powerful, complex and subtle—that terrified Mr. Adams.

In another sense, however, the mission of the College of Arts & Sciences is far less time-bound, and less transitory. At the most fundamental level, our job is familiar enough: we receive our first-year students—at eighteen and nineteen still adolescents—and we work with them as they grow, turning twenty, twenty-one, twenty-two. When they leave Grounds, I hope they will leave as better human beings than when they entered: more aware, ethical, compassionate— more like Henry Adams.

In their four years our first-year students will learn how to think for themselves, and above all, to think critically. I hope they will learn how to examine their assumptions and behaviors, and that these reflections will guide their every action.

The first-year students now join a community larger than they have known in their lives. In that exhilarating and often bewildering context, they will have to learn how to be both straightforward and nuanced in their relationship to the community: not just to go along and get along, but to grasp the complexity and genius of human relationships, how to build them, how to sustain them—also when to repair them and when to step back from them—and how to end them when they become destructive.

Henry Adams marveled that Virginians had the finest social instincts; he admired their irresistible grace and generosity. As Virginians—and Virginians in the larger sense that I have used the term today—this is our virtue. It is not ours alone, but one we identify with, a virtue we will always husband and uphold.

In the next four years our new students will not always experience the kind of hopes and aspirations and possibilities they feel today. There will be times of loneliness, uncertainty, doubt—and even a terrifying sense that the only thing inevitable and predictable is failure. These are the pangs of growth, of moving from adolescence to adulthood. In those moments, we will do our best—faculty, staff, fellow students—to be present, providing support, guidance, and advice. But there are limits to the College being "in loco parentis," the Latin phrase for "in the place of parents." The task of educating our Virginians here today extends then beyond the College and includes their parents—their active participation, dialogue, and constant communication with their children.

No matter how big the College may seem, its soul remains an intimate one, cloistered around hearth and home, visually represented by the Lawn, the Rotunda, the pavilions and the little rooms in between. Today we celebrate the birth of new members of our extended family, working toward the singular goal of taking from Virginia the best four years of their lives, striding confidently into the future beyond the Lawn.

64

COMMON SENSE EDUCATION— OR RULES OF THUMB FOR LIFE

GEORGE SANTAYANA, ONE of America's greatest philosophers, was also one of its finest cultural observers. In an essay that discusses materialism and idealism in American life, he describes an encounter with the president of Harvard, where he had long been on the faculty. As they walked together, the president asked Santayana how his classes were going. Santayana said fine—the students are intelligent and keen. The president stopped, turned to Santayana, and said, "I meant, how many students are in your classes."

Santayana used this as an example of the American penchant for reducing all things to the common denominator of quantity—presumably because numbers don't lie: How many tons of steel are produced in Bethlehem? How many miles of pavement are in New York? One hundred years after this encounter, we are even more beholden to what we might call the quantity theory of quality as a means to measure our value as teachers and scholars. I am sympathetic to all this, and admit to obsessing about the cost per student of instruction in subjects where demand is not strong—like one of the Less Commonly Taught Languages, or LCTLs, as they are known in the trade.

But it is also undeniably true that this focus on quantity has a silent partner or counterpart, which Santayana termed "diffidence as to quality." We should not be diffident. Quality, for all its resistance to measurement, should still be paramount. Maintaining and enhancing it is the core of what we must do.

When you take leave of your children this weekend, it is with the expectation that the University will provide skills that will place them in advantageous positions in life. But if you are like me—and I am a parent of a child leaving for college next week—you are also hoping for that ineffable thing that is difficult to measure and impossible to describe: an education in quality.

As your children spend the next four years in college, they will go from adolescents to adults over perhaps the most consequential four years of their lives, those years from eighteen to twenty-two. And you and I hope that they will mature as human beings, that they will learn to accurately gauge both the extent of the abilities we will provide them, as well as the limits imposed by circumstance. This is a kind of intelligence that has its roots in the context of events, in the realm of the real, and that manifests itself in the ability to align the complex aspects of reality and the limitless possibilities of the human mind. We might call these rules of thumb for life.

Santayana defined this kind of intelligence as "a certain shrewd orthodoxy which the sentiment and practice of laymen maintain everywhere." It encompassed "the current imagination and good sense of mankind—something traditional, conventional, incoherent, and largely erroneous ... yet something ingenious, practically acceptable, fundamentally sound, and capable of correcting its own errors." He said that there was something in the practicality of this human orthodoxy that struck him as poetical, catching the rhythm of the heart. It was the finely honed intelligence of everyman, and it was not something that could only be forged in Harvard Yard.

George Santayana, you may already know, was a Castilian aristocrat, and what caught the rhythm of his heart was, in my view, what we might call "common sense." So today, I would like to discuss with you the possibility that "common sense," something we often think of as innate, and therefore a gift rather than a product of assiduous cultivation, may indeed be one of the goals of college education—perhaps a prime goal.

This is also the subject of an extraordinary book, Common

Sense: A Political History, by one of our faculty in the College of Arts & Sciences, Sophia Rosenfeld. We think of common sense as the great attribute of Americans; in fact the most famous book by this title, Thomas Paine's 1776 Common Sense, was a publishing phenomenon, selling more than 100,000 copies in the first year alone. ("Common Sense for eighteen pence" was one of the great advertising slogans of the eighteenth century.)

As Professor Rosenfeld explains, however, "common sense" is a very old term, with a complex history. Aristotle thought of it as a nexus at the intersection of the five senses—vision, hearing, taste, smell, and touch. Others, like the Persian philosopher Avicenna, thought that common sense was the fundamental link between reason and the sensations, residing in the front of the first cerebral ventricle—in close proximity to its partner, imagination. For him, common sense was the cognitive faculty most vital to the discernment and judgment of character—of people, and circumstances—a kind of uncanny insight into the nature, possibilities, and trajectories of events. This is, no doubt, a function of experience and maturity—a healthy dose of which we seek to provide along that critical pathway between eighteen and twenty two.

Common sense is also "the sense that founds community." Here, "common" is used in the sense of shared, as in the shared tradition, a social virtue that holds society together. Professor Rosenfeld invokes modern intellectual traditions from Giambattista Vico down to the postwar German philosophers, in seeing in common sense—or, sensus communis, the sense of a community—the force that fundamentally shapes the moral and political existence of humanity. It is the product of life experience in community that affirms our connections to others, and that enables us to discern the common good.

Common sense, both in the sense of shrewd intelligence (which, through the maturity and encouragement of the community, brings the finest of our sensibilities together) and in the sense of tradition that founds and holds that community together, is then a virtue we must foster.

In The Genteel Tradition in American Philosophy, Santayana described American power and strength in terms of a genteel tradition that emanates from the shared tradition of Puritan New England on the one hand, and on the other, the young America—"originally composed of all the prodigals, truants, and adventurous spirits that the colonial families produced." Puritanism was accepted by "all the unkempt polyglot peoples that turn to the new world," forging the will to work and to prosper, as they inhabited this spacious and half-empty world. But if Puritanism was original to the creed, it was common sense, practicality, and the knowledge of everyday things, which would become the more long-lasting virtue. Famously, he said that the American Intellect inhabits the colonial mansion, and American Will, the skyscraper. And it is this vital tension between core values and ethics on the one hand, and ambition in the real world on the other, that is responsible for the dynamism and stability of American society.

It is also the tension that seems to have snapped in recent years. Americans are not an ideological people. We live in the determinate world of skyscraper heights and pavement miles—how many students are in your classes. Yet American politics has become curiously ideological. We can't have debt—even though quantitatively, our debt almost equals our GDP. Government is the problem. Government is not the problem. Left out is what might be called the efficacy of the real, of common sense—an ethic of solving problems pragmatically.

American education is an emporium of knowledge. It has long been a province of intellectualism but not necessarily of the kind of shrewd intelligence associated with common sense. But without the good common sense that is skeptical of large and unfounded claims and doctrines, without shared traditions that impel a society toward getting things done, it is increasingly difficult to hold America together.

Therefore I would hope that the education we provide your children over the next four years is—along with all the expert training we provide in terms of skill, technique, and method—also an education in common sense. As the repository of liberal arts education, our goal is to help refine the sensibilities of your children, but also to reinforce, in a properly respectful manner, the traditions and norms that the University of Virginia has shared and cherished. These began with a highly educated but eminently practical man: Thomas Jefferson.

The soldiers in the frontline of duty for that task are our faculty advisors, who are gathered here in the front of the auditorium. They are as excellent a team of advisors as you are likely to encounter in American higher education: experienced, professional, and above all, dedicated. So without further ado, let me introduce them.

MONEY ON THE LIBERAL ARTS

72

AT AN ACADEMIC panel in Atlanta on the morning of the Virginia-Auburn bowl game, an alumnus posed a question that has been posed many times, and with increasing frequency: Given all the national emphasis on the STEM disciplines (Science, Technology, Engineering, and Math), what did I think was the prospect for the liberal arts at the University of Virginia?

The short answer to the question is simple: ours is the College and Graduate School of Arts and Sciences, and we produce more STEM majors than any school in the University. One third of all students in the College graduate with majors (either single or double) in the sciences. This includes Psychology, which at U.Va. tends to be heavily experimental and neuroscience-oriented.

This liberal arts tradition has a long and venerable pedigree, going back hundreds of years. The medieval concept of the artes liberalis counted seven areas of requisite learning for a "free man" (the Latin liber meaning "free") with three arts focusing largely on facility with language—grammar, oratory, and logic—and four that are broadly mathematical—geometry, arithmetic, music, and astronomy.

One of the best modern examples of this venerable tradition is the liberal arts curriculum built around the Great Books, those considered the sine qua non for every educated person, as famously advocated at the University of Chicago from the 1930s onward. They were to be taught in small class settings, using primary or original materials, with give-and-take discussions rather than lectures, almost always on interdisciplinary subjects. While elsewhere the structure of the undergraduate curriculum nationally has oscillated back and forth like a metronome between the importance of requirements versus electives, Chicago still mandates two years of required courses for freshmen and sophomores. At Virginia the liberal arts remain a comprehensive curriculum that privileges the study of the arts and sciences, while continuing to differentiate itself from artes illiberalis or artes mechanicae, training in technical or vocational skills.

Yet, that still does not answer the question that our alumnus posed in Atlanta. When all is said and done, I don't think proponents of the liberal arts have done a good job articulating the mission of artes liberalis. Part of the problem is that the value of the intelligence that the liberal arts seek to foster is largely immeasurable and unquantifiable. If one agreed that the liberal arts are aimed at creating a "free man" (whoever this person is), what kind of intelligence characterizes him? What is he or she qualified to do with this intelligence?

These questions are particularly vexing in our country. The American public has never been comfortable with the notion of the life of the mind as a virtue in and of itself. The sociologist Richard Hofstadter in his Pulitzer Prize-winning book, Anti-Intellectualism in American Life, placed resentment and suspicion of the life of the mind (as well as the disposition to minimize its value) at the core of the American character. The distrust of the intellectual is the obverse of the American tendency to celebrate practical success. Looked at this way, anxiety about the liberal arts is nothing new; it is a recurring problem in American life.

At the core of this tension, Hofstadter argued, is the different place reserved in the American imagination for what he calls intellect on the one hand, and intelligence on the other. He defines intellect as the "critical, creative, and contemplative side of the mind," that constantly "examines, ponders, wonders, theorizes, criticizes, [and] imagines." Intelligence, on the other hand, "seeks to grasp, manipulate, re-order, and adjust," and will seize the immediate meaning in a situation and evaluate it. Americans have long admired the traits of intelligence, but showed ambivalence toward intellect. An innovator like Henry Ford would be a good example of applied intelligence, even if his intellect left something to be desired. Steve Jobs is a more recent example: a brilliant innovator, knowing what consumers would want before the product even existed, and then designing those products with great style and panache. But in all the deserved encomiums to him after he passed away, few put their finger on lasting ideas that might define his intellect, or the contemplative side of his mind, a mélange of Eastern and Western ideas typical of so many of his generation.

This distinction between intellect and intelligence is interesting, and it goes a long way to explain the complexity of American attitudes and the fluctuations in the public's relationship with the academy—and, in particular, the liberal arts. The American public might silently, sometimes grudgingly, admire intellect for its learned dignity, but may be all too quick to poke fun at "the eggheads," as they were called in Hofstadter's time.

The College of Arts and Sciences, more than any other unit in the University, is a place where intellect and intelligence commingle in a complex ebb and flow. Even Thomas Jefferson, duly renowned for both his intellect and his intelligence, would fluctuate in his estimation of the scholar versus the common man. In a letter to his nephew, Peter Carr, he wrote in 1787: "State a moral case to a plough man and a professor. The former will decide it as well, and often better than the latter because he has not been led astray by artificial rules." The "artificial rules" might suggest not ideas but abstruse dogma, whereas the plough man's ideas are, perhaps, rules of thumb that an intellectual would not recognize. Jefferson's felicitous expression "the useful science" suggests that he did not see the two approaches as mutually exclusive.

A similar call for combining the intellect and the intelligence was made in 1837 by Ralph Waldo Emerson in "The American Scholar," an essay often thought to be America's intellectual Declaration of Independence. The education of the scholar was not through books alone, he said, but through the resources we have inherited from our childhood—and through the influence upon the mind of nature: "Everyday, the sun: and after sunset, night and her stars. Ever the winds blow; ever the grass grows. Everyday, men and women, conversing, beholding and beholden. The scholar is he of all men who this spectacle most engages. . . . The mind now thinks; now acts; and each fit reproduces the other." In the right state, he is, "Man Thinking," and in the degenerate state, he becomes a "mere thinker." "Man Thinking" is the human in his environment; the "mere thinker" contemplates the world from his study, rarely leaving it.

How do we create this "right state," such that the American scholar is "Man Thinking," reflecting the best mix of intellect and intelligence? One important factor is something that seems far removed from both intellect and intelligence:

money. Lionel Trilling observed that in many civilizations there comes a point when wealth prefers the rule and company of mind and imagination. And he went on to compare intellect with money—both circulate and change, the value placed on both fluctuates (sometimes radically), both are conceptually hard to define, both are fluent and fluid. For Trilling, intellect and money are not simply similar, they are symbiotic: "money finds that it needs intellect, just as intellect finds that it needs money." But, he suggested, the relationship between money and intellect may be hard to fathom; they may be unaware of each other and their similarities, making it easy for an opposition to develop between them.

Please note: this equation of money and intellect is not a pitch for liberal arts fundraising. My point instead is that now is one of those times when the money and the intellect may be finding themselves in opposition. Good business practices and the argot of economics are as influential in academe as they have ever been, with a huge increase in the number of administrators and much self-examination about efficiency and productivity in both teaching and scholarship. These are important concerns, but it is also well worth remembering that the best teaching and scholarship produce, first and foremost, both intellect and intelligence.

My money is still on the liberal arts. Somehow in a country privileging knowledge—and increasingly, information—that is practical, utilitarian, and instrumental, the American intellect that Emerson exalted continues to survive and even flourish.

MORE
LIKE US

LIKE SO MANY, both inside and outside the academy, I tend to mark the passage of time by the books I read. For me, the 1980s opened with a book by Ezra Vogel, entitled "Japan as Number One," which foreshadowed all the worries about our loss of industrial supremacy that would come to haunt that troubled decade. In the book Japan seemed superior to America in every way: its government and corporations were as efficient as they were efficacious, increasing productivity while preserving social welfare; its politicians reigned over a stable polity as its bureaucrats wisely figured out everything from controlling crime to alleviating the energy shortage and reducing pollution. Meanwhile, its citizens were highly educated, amid all the uproar about why Johnny can't read—and Fumiko can.

By the end of the decade the country had grown weary of hearing about what was wrong with us, and wanted some assurance that uncultured, inefficient, and undereducated as we might be, we still had our heads screwed on right where our fundamental values were concerned: our liberalism, our democracy, our respect for privacy, and individualism. A perfect expression of this new zeitgeist was a book by James Fallows, called "More Like Us" (1989). That book, in my view, marked the end of the 1980s and ushered in the 1990s. The book celebrated American virtues—individualism, creativity, that can-do attitude—and turned every sow's ear in American culture into a silk purse: if our social order was disorderly, it was because we had a "talent for disorder," the sine qua non for creative excellence; every misstep was an opportunity to improve ourselves because America was a country of second chances, a forgiving culture. A prescient work by one irritated man, the book heralded what could only be described as the roaring '90s, as the microelectronics revolution, engineered and fueled by the collective talents of can-do and derring-do geeky pioneers, many of them immigrants, rode the crest of a flood of innovation that soon transformed our economy, with huge leaps in productivity—leaving Japan in the dust. Soon Japan slid into the economic doldrums that have continued to this day.

The jaw-dropping recall of Toyota vehicles in the past month, the largest recall in automotive history, makes one ponder the meaning of Number One. Japan wanted to be number one, and with Toyota, it did become the number one carmaker in the world, surpassing General Motors, which had held pride of place for nearly eighty years. Toyota wasn't simply big, it was profitable; just as the news of massive recalls were hitting the media, it announced that it was expecting to post a $900 million profit for the year that ends in March (a figure that will surely be revised). The irony is not lost on those of the reading public who came of age in the 1980s. In 1986, David Halberstam, the Pulitzer-winning reporter, best known for his book on the early days of the Vietnam War, "The Best and the Brightest," wrote a door-stopper of a book called "The Reckoning," a magisterial history of automobile firms in Japan and the United States. The trouble with the American automakers, he argued, was that their executives came from finance, not the assembly line, were obsessed with the bottom line, and always had one eye on the stock market. In contrast, their Japanese counterparts hailed from the ranks of engineers, knew the business of manufacturing machines down to the marrow of their bones, and both understood and were committed to quality. If Halberstam were alive today (he died in an automobile accident in 2007), he would say that race is not to the swift, but "the reckoning" happens to us all.

Until the Congressional hearings, we won't know whether

or not the Japanese have become more like Detroit over the years, putting profit over quality; even then, we may never know, since a modern car is an infernally complex beast on wheels with as many as a hundred microprocessor-controlled devices. "Quality control" is far more complicated today than it was a quarter century ago when Halberstam was looking under the Japanese hood.

What is undoubtedly true is that it takes more than a good product and the largest market share (or becoming the largest auto market, as China is now is) to become and to remain Number One. It takes leadership, entrepreneurship, accountability, and the ability to communicate—not just to a national but to a global audience. As the bad news began breaking, the flustered chairman of Toyota finally held a brief news conference—on a Friday evening, in a place two hours from Tokyo—hoping to shake off the journalists beating down his door. He said nothing new and communicated nothing, only a formulaic apology devoid of meaning. He might as well have been the Roger Smith character in Michael Moore's "Roger and Me," the emblem of shirked accountability for the ruin of the city that Buick built, Flint, Michigan. It is a sad irony that the first indication of the current Toyota trouble can be traced to Flint, where a 77-year-old former GM employee was driving a 2005 Toyota Camry when the accelerator stuck. She died in the ensuing collision with a tree.

To be Number One, James Fallows argued that we had to remember how to be "more like us," and less like Japan—or

China, or Asia. As he extolled and recounted the virtues of this country, virtues hidden in the shadow of all the sack-cloth and ashes of the 1980s, he also condemned what he said were the Asian qualities that were seeping into the American culture, compromising its entrepreneurial spirit. He called it the Confucianization of America, meaning the meritocratic tendency centered on examinations and credentials, fostering excessive competition.

Leaving aside the accuracy of this caricature of Asian education, there is perhaps something to the argument that we as a nation have become excessively focused on credentials. Here at the College, I sometimes discern this tendency in the steadily upward trend in multiple majors over the past decade. The requirements for more than one major can be strenuous, crowding out the flexibility for students to venture out to new fields, experiment in ways that push the limits of knowledge. In the College, we offer some three thousand course sections, and I wonder whether something essential is lost when students trade in a broad liberal arts curriculum in order to satisfy the new requirements for an additional credential.

Regardless of whether students graduate with one major or two, it remains a fact that our educational system is the best in the world. And regardless of who is number one in auto sales, it is our educational system that is our best comparative advantage. It keeps foreign students flocking to our shores, especially from Asia. In the long run, these students will, in one way or another, be more like us, and I think they will be better for it.

THE PRICE OF INSPIRATION

LAST WEEK I RECEIVED a letter from an anguished parent, distressed about the study-abroad fees levied on U.Va. students attending non-U.Va. programs. (There are fewer fees for students participating U.Va.-sponsored programs abroad.) To study in Freiburg, Germany this spring, his daughter had to pay two administrative fees that added up to $550 plus an application fee of $90; to study art in Italy this summer, she was asked to pay yet another $400 in administrative fees, plus another application fee of $90. The total came to $1,130—not a trivial sum, especially coming on the heels of other hidden costs associated with transplanting a child to Europe.

I should know. My son is about to commence his study abroad in Berlin, and I am stunned by the dizzying array of costs associated with ensconcing a child in a foreign country. After paying various fees to the University of Chicago where he is a student, and the extra cost of language school and home-stay, we also laid out cash for his survival fees—a new cell phone for local use; the chargers he needs (and always forgets) for the many gadgets he can't live without; new subway cards and rail tickets; a new pair of Birkenstocks; books, dictionaries, and other supplies. It is as if you pay to start college all over again. Then there are the great museums and concerts that beckoned him to Berlin in the first place, and that must be appreciated; the cafes and beer gardens; the choucroute, flammekuche, and endless sausages to choose from; and of course, all the cities to be explored—each of which costs money, at a time when the dollar remains weak against the euro.

The charge that the anguished parent found most galling was the $400 administrative fee, recently mandated by the Board of Visitors, which was required for his daughter to take her studio art class in Italy. I wrote to explain that the $400 covers the administrative costs of approving non-U. Va. programs and credit transfer, financial aid packaging/repackaging, advising services, pre-departure orientations and emergency response to student needs while abroad—and then I sheepishly added that at $400, we were a bargain, compared to University of North Carolina's $650. I know that this was no consolation to him.

In truth, however, the "cost" of education, either on Grounds or abroad, cannot be computed. Unlike a for-profit business, we run a money-losing operation. U.Va., like other excellent colleges and universities, provides a cornucopia of services that cost far more than what it charges, and it subsidizes the loss through its state appropriations, endowments and funds from gifts and bequests from alumni and other private donors. Even if U.Va. charged its students the full cost of their education, the fact remains that there is really no meaningful way to express in monetary terms the benefits of learning.

On the third day my son arrived in Berlin, he paid 49 euro for a bus trip to Dresden. His guide who, like so many Berliners, said he was "completing [his] dissertation," took him to Frauenkirche, the domed church which had graced Dresden's skyline for two centuries before it collapsed after the infamous firebombing of the city. "There were three thousand bombers covering the sky on that day in February 1945, and the people ran out to the street to find out what this was all about," the guide said, as he squinted his eyes against the brilliant August sun and let out a long sigh. "Dresden has never been a city prepared for tragedy." But it is prepared for rebirth: after the reunification, a grass-roots movement arose to painstakingly rebuild Frauenkirche, and to make whole the rubble and fragments of a city as stunningly beautiful as it was defenseless. It was a big lesson in just one day, for 49 euros.

TO THE PARENTS OF INCOMING CLASS

LAST WEEKEND I GREETED many of you who were fortunate enough to accompany your children to Charlottesville and help them move in as they start a new and important phase of their life. For those parents I was not able to meet, let me offer my greetings in print, as Dean of the College and Graduate School of Arts and Sciences, but also as another parent. The older of my two children is starting his third year in a university in Chicago; so two years ago, I was in the same situation you are in, sending off a child to be on his own.

During the convocation at his university, I sat—like so many of you did last Friday—and listened to no less than four different administrators speak about the "life of the mind," and about the fabled discussions in the student dormitories that stretch into the wee hours of the night at that university—as students debate about Adorno and Horkheimer, about Foucault and Poulantzas. That is certainly admirable—far better that they should contemplate the horrors of the historical predicaments that Adorno and Horkheimer faced, than to spend hours on Facebook with ear phones jammed into their heads, rap music pulsating in their brains. They will do enough of that, as all parents know.

Today, however, I want to talk to you about something other than the "life of the mind," another kind of life. Exactly one hundred years ago, Abbott Lawrence Lowell, who was then President of Harvard, said: "The object of the undergraduate education is not to produce hermits, each imprisoned in the cell of his own intellectual pursuits, but men fitted to take their places in the community and live in contact with their fellowman." What he said was true then, and it is true today, and it includes both men and women.

I am mindful that you have entrusted us with an exquisite responsibility—to educate, nurture, and help find larger purposes in life for your children, who are dearer to you than life itself. In the four years that your children will be with us, they will transition from being male-children to men, and female-children to women. Those will be truly complicated years—exhilarating, challenging, confusing, frightening, and fraught with massive opportunities and dangers. The College will provide your children with safe boundaries in which they can grow, learn, experiment, and find out who they are as human beings. And at the end of the four years, your child will leave Charlottesville better educated and more mature—and above all, a better human being.

In Aristotle's Politics, he pondered the purpose of education. Do we as educators impart to our students truth through knowledge, or do we impart useful skills? Or—and here is a tough one—do we impart virtue? There are many professors who believe that truth, being relative, cannot be taught, let alone virtue. Yet the point of our education really ought to be all three: knowledge, skills, and virtue, each informing the other.

But how do you teach virtue?

Harry Lewis, a former dean at Harvard, reminds us in his recent and excellent book Excellence without a Soul, what John Dewey said about learning: "the only way to develop curiosity, sympathy, principle, and independence of mind is to practice being curious, sympathetic, principled, and independent. For those of us who are teachers, it isn't what we teach that instills virtue; it is how we teach. We are the books our students read most closely."

At the College of Arts and Sciences, we still practice something that has gone out the window at most research universities: faculty advising. We are one of the last public universities where world famous scholars—Guggenheim award winners, members of national academies—are still assigned undergraduate advisees; and where mentoring takes places at every level—in residence halls, classrooms small and large, tutorials, undergraduate research opportunities, and in the pavilions on the lawn where the deans live, just as Mr. Jefferson intended.

Our system of mentoring and advising is not perfect, and it is stretched to the limit. It is hard to ask excellent scholars to dedicate themselves to advising when few other research institutions would insist that they do so. And it is not necessarily the case that world-class researchers make the best advisors and mentors. But we do what we can, with an imperfect system—and always trying to make it better. We have no choice: as the teachers of your children, we are the books your children read most closely, and we will endeavor to be better role models.

For your part, I would ask that you stay in touch with your children. I don't mean that you should hover over them as "helicopter parents," but please stay in touch, which is so easy to do these days with cell phones, text messages, email, and even Facebook pages that many of you keep. No matter how safe we try to keep the confines of your children's universe for the next four years, there are always dangers—like drugs and excessive alcohol, the scourges that afflict every university.

I would also ask you to be engaged with the College. You

have every right to scrutinize our work, and we are the better for it. If you have any questions, do not hesitate to email me at mwoo@virginia.edu. I don't have all the answers, but I know the deans and faculty members and administrators who do, and we will answer your queries as efficiently as we can, and do our best to help you and your children.

Welcome. I cannot tell you how delighted I am that you are now part of the College community.

BACK TO THE SHORES OF TRIPOLI: LESSONS OF 9/11

THE MAGIC OF YOUTH can transform a nightmare into a memory. Over the past weekend, the students and the University commemorated the ten-year anniversary of the 9/11 attacks with a dizzying array of events—speeches, conferences, exhibits, interfaith dialogues, flag runs, and candlelight vigils. Ubiquitous on the Grounds were students wearing yellow ribbons: we remember 9/11.

Magic, indeed, because this is truly a melancholy ten-year anniversary. Ten years later, we are a nation at war in

Afghanistan, Iraq, and Libya. Defense spending in constant dollars is at its highest level since World War II. Meanwhile, according to new Census Bureau information, poverty levels in the U.S. are at a 52-year high, and nearly 50 million Americans between the ages of 18 and 64 have not worked in the past year. One in five children live below the poverty line. Official unemployment has remained over 9 percent for years, and that includes only those who have not given up actively seeking work. Meanwhile, our leaders in Washington cannot agree on the problems that beset the country, and new political movements decry government involvement in social welfare, the bipartisan approach since 1933.

Looking back to 2001, Mel Leffler, a distinguished diplomatic historian in the College, argued in the current issue of Foreign Affairs that the tragedy of 9/11, among others, was an opportunity missed. In spite of campaign talk about a reinvigorated, strong defense establishment, George W. Bush was a president who, on the eve of 9/11, was focused on his domestic agenda: tax cuts, education reform, faith-based voluntarism, and energy policy. Then the disaster struck and a momentary national unity dissolved into endless conflict and bickering, over the Iraq War, over the 2008 financial crisis, and on and on. Most Americans seem fed up with Washington in particular and politicians in general.

It thus appears that 2001 was the beginning of a decade that finds us where we are today—disillusioned, dismayed, discomfited. Paradoxically, though, the second decade of this century has opened with major rays of hope in the form of the "Arab Spring" that began earlier this year. This modern political movement that has nothing to do with terrorism has made Al Qaeda's antediluvian calls for a new Islamic Caliphate finally appear as anachronistic as they in fact are. The Arab Spring extended into late summer when a NATO coalition helped Libyans overthrow the Qadaffi regime. The rebels took control of the capital almost exactly on the 9/11 anniversary—a victory on the shores of Tripoli.

Unbeknownst to most Americans, 2001 also marked the two hundred year anniversary of a war that offers telling parallels to the current war in Libya, and a possible path toward reimagining our foreign relations in the twentieth-first century. I am thinking about the first Barbary War, fought "on the shores of Tripoli" (hence the phrase in the Marine anthem). The president at the time was Thomas Jefferson. It was the only war that he executed during his presidency, and he did so with his characteristic wisdom, courage and brilliance. It was an excellent example of the judicious conduct of foreign affairs, encountering unfamiliar enemies with unfamiliar beliefs in far away lands, but "getting the job done" without entangling Americans in their domestic affairs—or causing a civil war among Libyan tribes.

Within three months of his inauguration, Jefferson found himself in a war with the Pasha of Tripoli. As Henry Adams tells the story in his magnificent study of the presidencies of Jefferson and Madison, from time immemorial the northern coast of Africa had been occupied by pirates who "figured in the story of Don Quixote as in the lies of Scapin, and enlivened with picturesque barbarism the semi-civilization of European habits and manners through centuries of slow growth." The four Barbary Powers – Morocco, Algiers, Tunis, and Tripoli – lived on blackmail. The United States, like nations in Europe, had purchased safe passage with all four powers, and in the ten years preceding the inauguration of Jefferson, had paid more than two million dollars in ransom, gifts, and tribute. However, when the new president rebuffed additional extortions from the Pasha of Tripoli on May 14, 1801, he declared war on the U.S. and chopped down the flagstaff that stood in front of the American Consulate. Algiers, Tunis, and Morocco were also clamoring for more tribute; there was reason to believe that they might make common cause with Tripoli.

The pirates were not worthy enemies, of course, and, according to Jefferson's detractors, their defeat was not worth deploying expensive new frigates. Still, something had to be done to bring an end to a century and a half of piracy. And so over the next four years, in what Jefferson laconically described as a "cruise," his navy and newly-created Marines bombarded and attacked the harbors of northern Africa. The USS Argus, Chesapeake, Constellation, Constitution (not yet dubbed "Old Ironsides"), Enterprise, Intrepid, Philadelphia, and Syren all saw service during this war, under the overall command of Commodore Edward Preble.

The regime in Tripoli, however, remained defiant and even succeeded in capturing the USS Philadelphia in 1803. The blackmailers feared that if they buckled under foreign pressure, their own subjects might revolt. In 1804, in the most heroic episode of the Barbary War, Captain Stephen Decatur Jr. sailed into Tripoli, set fire to the captured Philadelphia (to deny her use to the enemy), rescued the crew from imprisonment, bombarded the fortified town, and boarded the Pasha's fleet at anchor, in what Lord Nelson himself would call "the most bold and daring act of the age."

As the summer of 1805 approached, however, despite the success of the naval action and blockade, it was still not clear that the Pasha would sue for peace. William Bainbridge, the captain of the Philadelphia, believed that President Jefferson had to choose between paying a ransom in gold or blood. He thought it would take ten thousand troops to take the Pasha's castle in Tripoli.

As it turned out, victory was won without invasion. William Eaton, a Connecticut Yankee with a classical education at Dartmouth, was hell-bent on regime change in Tripoli by whatever means necessary. No fan of Thomas Jefferson, he scoffed at the idea of a political millennium "ushered in upon us as the irresistible consequence of the goodness of heart, integrity of mind, and correctness of disposition of Mr. Jefferson," and ridiculed the notion that "all nations, even pirates and savages, were to be moved by the influence of his persuasive virtue and masterly skill in diplomacy."

As T. E. Lawrence would do in Arabia a century later, Eaton put himself at the head of a most improbable army. As Adams writes, "so motley a horde of Americans, Greeks, Tripolitans and Arab camel-drivers had never before been seen on the soil of Egypt." Eaton led his mercenaries across five hundred miles of desert until they reached the city of Derne. Three American cruisers bombarded from the sea as Eaton and his men stormed the walls of the harbor fortress and took the city. After a failed attempt to win it back, the Pasha finally threw in the towel.

The battle on the shores of Tripoli was the first time that US Marines fought on foreign soil. It would not be the last. Still, there are lessons to be learned. The limited objectives that Jefferson pursued are a pristine example of what the political theorist and philosopher Michael Walzer has called a "just war," in the modern sense. It was a war with all the requisites: it began in self-defense, it had a good cause and right intention, a high probability of success, and the important measure of proportionality. Finally, war came as the last resort, after both bribery and diplomacy had failed. It was also modern in a less edifying sense: Jefferson did not request a declaration of war from Congress.

Apart from that lapse, which now seems routine (no American president since 1941 has gone to war according to the provisions of the Constitution), the Barbary War had a moral basis that goes beyond attacking terrorists, which the pirates certainly also were. Between 1530 and 1780, over one million

Europeans and Americans were enslaved in Islamic North Africa, captured by pirates whose corsairs raided as far north as England and Ireland; in 1631, in the famous "sack of Baltimore" an entire Irish village disappeared into slavery in a single night.

A proportional response to the havoc caused by the terrorists on the fateful day of 9/11 was to capture and punish those who perpetrated the act—as we eventually did ten years later, picking off Osama bin Laden in his hideout in Pakistan, a stealthy and successful action that spilled as little blood as possible, using not local mercenaries but a small, coherent, highly-trained force of Navy SEALS. Across the border in Afghanistan, ten years after 2001, our efforts to dislodge the Taliban and deny a haven to Al Qaeda still grinds on, with 100,000 American boots on the ground.

Somehow, our strategy in Libya seems more Jeffersonian: the limited use of force (in this case to save civilian lives), support for a modern (and we hope democratic) movement against dictatorship, limited objectives, and keeping American boots off the ground. The Arab Spring has brought forth reasons to hope that the future will be better than the decade-long remains of that terrible September day.

97

II

PLACE

LIVING ON
THE LAWN

LAST MONTH MY FAMILY moved into Pavilion II, the house that abuts the Rotunda on the east side (the right as you face the Rotunda). This elegant and unassuming house is a gateway that connects two very different worlds, in the most beguiling ways. From the Lawn, perhaps America's most perfect physical expression of the universe of learning, one enters a house that is elegantly elongated, both vertically and horizontally, with light flooding in from its triple-hung windows. Walking past the living room that our movers began calling "the ballroom" as they reassembled an old Schimmel piano there, and the dining room that leads to the back door, one arrives at a breathtaking vista that reveals what John Donne might have called "a little world cunningly made": sloping layers of garden that offer quiet refuge and solace from the hustle and bustle of academic life.

Sequestered by Mr. Jefferson's famous serpentine walls, the garden opens out to the fullness of the season. In the spring, the garden blazes with dogwood and azaleas, and then lilacs, followed by day lilies, lavender, and chaste trees, and the crepe myrtle, whose deep red seems even deeper on a hot summer day. The garden is as bountiful as it is beautiful, yielding fruit—fig, elderberry, apple, strawberry, blueberry and grape—as well as herbs, and all of this watched over by an ancient bigleaf magnolia, the type that produces large blossoms with a hint of yellow and purple at its center. One of these days the tree will have to be felled; but for now, it stands firm, insisting on bestowing dignity to a garden nearly two centuries old.

For moderns and postmoderns like us, the new house presents some special challenges. It is a house with significant history, and history is always a burden, even as one learns from it. In moving into the Pavilion, I did not have the freedom of the typical homeowner to do as I pleased— the kind of willful and rebellious ignorance one sometimes yearns for, and is politely denied, at the University of Virginia. Here we start our scholarly journey by learning the

101

meaning of the structures bequeathed to us.

Based on the Ionic style of the Temple of the Fortuna Virilis in Rome, as published by Palladio, the Pavilion has the distinguishing features of this order, such as a frieze of ox skulls, putti, ribbons, and garlands festooned with fruit motifs. The entablatures are visible outside over the columns as well in one of the rooms upstairs. Jefferson fretted over the last detail of the design, down to the quality and cost of the bricks with which to build this home. He did not live to see the first faculty move in, but he seems to have conceived it for the teaching of medicine. The first five inhabitants were physicians and medical school professors. It was not until 1896 that a non-physician—James Harris, professor of modern languages—moved in. Since then, availability and opportunity, rather than academic discipline, have determined the choice of inhabitants in Pavilion II.

102

For much of my adult life, I have been, by avocation, a restorer of old houses. Restoration of old homes is an act of love but also an obligation, to see to it that beautiful old structures with significant meaning are nursed back to life and their former glory, with modern amenities. Eventually I learned to greet all my contractors and subcontractors—all too many of them over the years—in their native languages, and together we restored old Midwestern houses built around time when industrialization was breathing new life into the prairie.

The interesting thing about "This Old House" called

Pavilion II is that it cannot be retrofitted for modernity, however thorough the renovation may have been. Rather, modernity gets retrofitted to accommodate the old house—and not just because it is utterly bereft of closets or its small kitchen does not allow cooking over a gas flame. Rather, the location and structure of the house harkens back to an earlier era that calls forth a conception of learning and social life different from what prevails in most research universities. Pavilion II is an integral part of learning and of the University's community, as it was conceived in the mind of its architect. It is not a place designed for withdrawal but for engagement; not for possessive individualism but for sharing—much like the nature of knowledge, which is useful only in the sharing and spreading of it. Pavilion II is my house as it is yours, a place that our students can come when they want to talk with their dean and a home away from home for our alumni.

In the garden, the camellias are in full bloom. Hugging the wall that separates the upper and lower gardens, the white flowers are unusually luminous on this Thanksgiving Day, throwing light to the garden otherwise dormant for the season. I don't know who planted those white camellias, a species that originated from my native region of East Asia, and one of my favorite flowers. But their presence strikes me as being emblematic of Pavilion II: inspired by the classical from around the world, alive to the present, looking to the future.

103

TOMMY
FOUR

THE SNOW BEGAN FALLING on the Lawn in the hours before dawn of Sunday, March 27. The voices of the students, strolling in twos and threes down the arcades, drifted up to my bedroom in the pavilion and then they grew faint. The snow fell all morning over the Grounds and through the afternoon. It fell silently on the trees that had been planted when the University was founded and in the years that have followed. I watched the snowflakes drifting through the branches of trees already in bloom—cherries, plums, Bradford pears, and

APRIL 2011

star magnolias—and those about to flower. I saw it falling on the daffodils, hyacinths, periwinkles, and Virginia bluebells, and all the brilliant forsythias. When the snow finally stopped, the day suddenly turned dark and cold, with a wind that bites hard into the flesh and into the bone. I remember hearing that with a cold snap like this, flowers may not produce fruit. I was vaguely troubled by what might happen to the white flowering quinces and apricots in the back, whether they might have been damaged. That night, Thomas West Gilliam IV, fondly referred to as "Tommy Four" by family and friends, scaled the roof of the Physics Building with friends. They wanted to take in the night view of the Grounds. Slipping on ice, Tommy fell forty feet to the ground.

Tommy was nineteen, soon to finish his first year in the College. He came from a large and close-knit family that was dispersed around the world. He was born in Texas, but had traversed the world with his parents. He lived in Australia (where to make the business of ethnic nomenclature more efficient, young Tommy once referred to himself as "Australian-American"); and for most of his teenage years, he lived in Dublin. His classmates at U.Va. called him "the guy from Ireland."

Tommy's mother, Vicki Gilliam, said that he fretted sometimes about leaving his friends behind in Dublin and having to make new friends at U.Va., something entirely understandable: "adjustments," and "fitting-in" are the cultural tropes of our children. But because he had been exposed from early on to the world beyond our borders, and loved the friends he made all over the world, he had a terrific advantage. It gave him an innate ability to empathize with others, to understand their "origins"—not merely in an ethnic and geographic sense, but in the sense of what Aristotle meant by the word nous, the intellectual origins and inclinations and sensibilities that guide human trajectories—to arrive finally at their mind's center.

In ENWR 1510—an argumentative writing class that focused on issues like aid to Africa, the trans-Atlantic drug trade and human trafficking—Tommy was an active participant, a tenacious debater with a steel-trap mind, the kind that professors love to have, and come to rely on, in class. Tommy knew more than other students, able to imagine and extrapolate on the basis of living abroad; and Tommy's presence, according to his teacher James Patterson, provided one of the "incentives for the students for attending class." (But it still did not prevent Tommy from leaving the class early one day to attend the U.Va.-Duke basketball game—whereupon the "Duke game" became a class joke for absences.)

Likewise, he was a good debater in the discussion section that Art Espey led in Introduction to International Relations. Had he been able to finish the next three years, he would most likely have majored in Foreign Affairs, like his uncle, Robert (College '91). Robert lives in Beirut, Lebanon. In French class, his teacher recalled Tommy's essay, written with remarkable fluency, about his dream of spending

Christmas in the French Alps, and of skiing during the day and playing games and watching classic holiday films in the evening. In that class, as in others, Tommy's teachers recalled his lilting Irish brogue.

Seamus Heaney, the Irish poet, said that poetry creates an order "where we can at least grow up to that which we stored up as we grew." All the things that surrounded Heaney as the eldest child in a large family in rural County Derry—rain in the trees, mice in the ceiling, a steam locomotive rumbling along the railway line one field back from his house, as he put it—formed the core of who he was, as our own surroundings form the core of who we are. He likened the distance between our human core and the adult world we inhabit to the drinking water that stood in a bucket in the scullery of his house: "every time a passing train made the earth quake, the surface of that water used to ripple delicately, concentrically, and in utter silence."

I met Tom Gilliam III (College '85, Darden '90) and Vicki on Tuesday after Tommy's accident. Vicki had flown in from Dublin that afternoon, and they were huddled with a few students in Pavilion V. Tom had majored in English before he went on to Darden, and like Tommy later on, he knew every corner of the Grounds intimately, and he reveled in sharing with his son all his affections for the College. On that Tuesday, however, Tom wasn't focused on himself or even Tommy. He was focused on the students in the room; they had been with Tommy when he fell to his death, or else

107

saw him in his last hour. They are in no way responsible for this accident, he said, and they must not let it, cruel and inexplicable as it is, compromise the innocence and joys of their days on the Grounds. As the students sobbed, Tom and Vicki comforted them; and in their compassion for other people's children, they seemed to have forgotten, if momentarily, the immensity of the catastrophe that had just befallen them.

Tommy's memorial service was unusual for one whose life was cut so short, and it overflowed with hundreds of people from everywhere in the world. They remembered a student on the cusp of manhood—handsome, radiant, intelligent, the kind that parents wish their daughters would marry. Tommy's aunt Connally (College '87, Curry '90) was there, and I met Tommy's uncle from Beirut who likes the College magazine that is delivered to his doorstep, and Tommy's grandfather who lives in Charlottesville, and who extended his gratitude for President Sullivan's kind words about Tommy.

I never taught Tommy, I never met him. But I have some sense of what he must have "stored up" as he grew, the influences of family, friends and places that formed his core—and the gentle ripples from and around it. It is not difficult to imagine the broadening paths of the marvelous life he would have had, and the impact he would have made on those around him. I wish we had him for another three years.

When Seamus Heaney received his Nobel Prize in Literature in 1995, he invoked the other great Irish poet who preceded him in Stockholm. In "The Municipal Gallery

Revisited," William Butler Yeats spoke of the impact that his friends, like Augusta Gregory and John Synge, had had on modern Irish history and himself:

> You that would judge me do not judge alone
> This book or that, come to this hallowed place
> Where my friends' portraits hang and look thereon;
> Ireland's history in their lineaments trace;
> Think where man's glory most begins and ends
> And say my glory was I had such friends.

The flowering quince in my backyard was damaged by the ice. And in Final Exercises three years from now, Tommy's voice won't mix in the roar that will burst into the air with hundreds of balloons. Yet this is where the glory of the University still begins and ends. Our glory was that we had Tommy—forever radiant and innocent in our mind's eye—and his large and boisterous family as our friends.

FOREVER YOUNG

IN 1975, MICK JAGGER said that if at 45 he were still singing "Satisfaction," he would shoot himself. At 67, he is still singing it, and Keith Richards is playing that famous three-note riff. They are slightly ahead of the Baby Boomers, harbingers of what is to come: a generation young in mind and consciousness even if old in body (or supernaturally re-silient, like Keith Richards).

Most of you graduated in 1961, a year of great promise, with "The New Frontier," the Peace Corps, and America at the height of its power. Within two years, John Kennedy was assassinated, the Vietnam War was underway, and the struggle for civil rights was rocking the nation.

If the '60s in America were an era of terrible dilemmas, they would also come to be seen as an age of "amorality"; to use a tired phrase, a time of sex, drugs, and rock-and-roll.

You, the Class of 1961, know better. The '60s were also a time of revolutionary thought, of boundless energy and discovery, when the culture of youth began its ascendancy and never looked back.

It was around this time that an idea crept into our consciousness, the idea that one can live agelessly.

So, it is not surprising that 50 years after you graduated, the notion of "amorality" that once branded you in your youth has been replaced with "amortality," the aspiration to keep aspiring, in the sense of breathing, to live the same way and enjoy the same things, perhaps not at the same pace, from your late teens to the day you die.

According to Time magazine, the people of the amortal era "rarely ask themselves if their behavior is age-appropriate, because that concept has little meaning for them. They don't structure their lives around the inevitability of death, because they prefer to ignore it. Instead, they continue to chase aspirations and covet new goods and services. Amortals assume all options are always open."

Hugh Hefner, whose fame is indelibly linked to the early 1960s and his "Playboy philosophy," is a classic amortal. He's preparing to marry a woman 60 years younger and once said that Viagra was invented with him in mind. Woody Allen no longer plays the much-older man wooing the young woman in his films (he was shamed out of it by his critics), but he is married to one. Elton John becomes a first-time dad at age 62. Keith Richards writes a fascinating memoir that sums up the essence of amortality: the spirit lives on while the body caves in. Women, too, like Madonna, challenge our notions of age-appropriate behavior.

These amortals don't just express the Zeitgeist, they embody the important truth that consciousness changes and evolves at a much different pace than the body does. Amortality characterizes an entire generation, the largest in American history, namely, the Boomers and their precursors. You see the world through 25-year-old eyes, even at 75, and imagine yourself still becoming the person you want to become. Instead of a fixed adult identity, you have instead a constant searching, and a becoming: the years slip by, but you still think of yourself as youthful. Your consciousness is forever young.

Muhammad Ali and Howard Cosell had a complicated relationship. But when Ali won the heavyweight championship for the third time, Cosell quoted Bob Dylan's song, "Forever Young." I have always liked that piece, especially the last stanza:

> May your hands always be busy
> May your feet always be swift
> May you have a strong foundation

When the winds of changes shift

May your heart always be joyful

And may your song always be sung

May you stay forever young.

The amortality of consciousness applies also to this university of yours, whose bicentennial we will celebrate in 2019. Most of you went to the College in the late 1950s—a world I glimpse now and then through the writings of my good friend, Ken Ringle, who, by the way, has returned today for his 50th reunion. Ken is a former writer for the Washington Post, and wrote a very funny recollection of William Faulkner's time at the University in 1958. Ken was stalking him in the hope of better understanding the Biblical allusions in Light in August, or the stained glass imagery in Go Down, Moses. While I don't know that he got anywhere, I liked his piece so much that I posted it on my blog.

Ken wrote another piece, called "The University in the Late Fifties." It's a socio-cultural history, shrewd as it comes, and politically incorrect about a time that was, by today's standards, politically incorrect. As he tells it, the students "drank bourbon over ice in the stands at football games, scotch and soda while bopping to blues bands in sweaty, smoke-filled fraternity houses, gin and juice and bloody marys on Sunday polo games … and lots of beer with meals." It was a time when many Virginia students owned firearms and kept them in their rooms—mostly shotguns or rifles for hunting. Ken recalls seeing a deer carcass hanging by its heels from the porch of Sigma Pi. There were WWII and Korean War veterans who would pack their .45 service revolvers on road trips and shoot out the gate lights at Sweet Briar. It was a time when most of the students, whether in-state or imported, had some sort of tie to the land, and before the University saw an avalanche of students from Northern Virginia. Of course, like the TV series "Mad Men," this still was a man's world, with little inkling of the gender and racial diversity that would soon inhabit the Grounds.

Ken remembers classmates whose parents sent them to Virginia because, after Harvard, it was "the only other socially acceptable school." After all, what other state university had a polo team? Ken also quoted the late CBS correspondent Charles Kuralt describing a Virginia diploma as "not only scholarly but patrician," a distinction that had always escaped Chapel Hill where Kuralt went to school. For up-wardly-mobile Irish Catholics named Kennedy (as in, Bobby and Ted) Harvard and Virginia were their preferred choices. If there is a consciousness of the University that remains forever young—from the founding of the University through the late 1950s, when so many of you went to school, down to the present day—I think it is this tension between aristocracy and populism: being a public Ivy, a state university with a polo team, a place that is at once patrician and democratic. To say that such essential tension defines who we are may seem elitist until we remember that this is exactly how Mr.

Jefferson would have intended us to grow.

He believed in a naturally occurring aristocracy of talent and virtue, liberally scattered across all segments of the population—including the poor and the uneducated. It was the role of the university to "cull from every condition of our people" this natural aristocracy and provide it with opportunity in the form of education. By marrying this aristocracy of talent to democracy, he signaled that the purpose of his university lies in the exquisite refinement of human sensibility, to serve our democratic citizenry. Only a renaissance man could have defined democratic education in this way.

The University and the College should be as recognizable to you today as it was to you then. It evolves and changes, often in dramatic ways as our contemporary diversity attests, but it retains a spirit and a tradition, instantly recognizable, telling us we could be nowhere else, on no other Grounds, at no other university. It is almost two centuries old, but it has its own amortality: it stays forever young in its consciousness and in its aspiration. It was as recognizable to Mr. Jefferson as it is to you and to me.

So, to Mr. Jefferson, to you, and to today's students at U.Va., let me raise a toast and recite the "Virginia Creed" (of unknown authorship):

"To be a Virginian, either by Birth, Marriage, Adoption, or even on one's Mother's Side, is an Introduction to any State in the Union, a Passport to any Foreign Country, and a Benediction from Above."

PITCH PERFECT

ON MAY 30, JIM TRESSEL, one of the most successful coaches in the history of Big Ten powerhouse Ohio State, resigned in the wake of an NCAA rules violations investigation. It was big news everywhere, but especially in Ohio, where college football couldn't possibly be any bigger. The Tressel episode is only the most recent case study on the perils of big-time sports at American universities. Storied football programs and the immense funding they both generate and require have put universities like Ohio State on the national map. Yet Derek Bok, the former president of Harvard, argued in a book titled "Universities in the Marketplace: The Commercialization of Higher Education" that college sports, long expected to boost alumni giving, are not in fact good money-makers, especially at universities not near the top of the national football rankings. Instead, Bok says, they exploit students who are often admitted with low grades and test scores and are then given too little time to study. Still, he adds, competition among universities and colleges has kept up the pressure for more aggressive athletic programs, often undermining their educational values.

Until three years ago when I came to U.Va., I was a Michigan fan, so I can't deny feeling a bit of schadenfreude at Tressel's demise. Under Tressel, the Buckeyes amassed a 9-1 record against their archrivals, the Wolverines, a better winning percentage than even the legendary Woody Hayes, who beat Michigan 16 times, but also lost 11 times, something that Buckeye fans somehow tend to forget.

On the same day that Tressel resigned, Virginia's men's lacrosse team won the national championship in Baltimore, defeating the University of Maryland. It was a beastly hot day, and the heat, rising from the artificial turf, turned the stadium into an inferno, with reported temperatures of 120 degrees on the field. The lacrosse championship was a great triumph, considering all the pain the team has had to endure this past year. For most of our fourth-year student-athletes, this was the last competitive lacrosse game they will play.

They will go on to graduate school, law school, business school, and other professional careers. They all have had superb guidance under veteran coach Dom Starsia, who has won four national championships at Virginia and was national coach of the year twice at Brown.

Meanwhile, the Virginia baseball team was beating North Carolina and then Florida State to win the ACC championship. At this writing, the team is on to this weekend's NCAA Super Regional, seeded number one in the nation.

My good friend Hugh Evans (College '88) played baseball during his time at U.Va. He told me that Wahoo baseball, like lacrosse, is a study in leadership. He recalled that U.Va. endured many sub-.500 seasons while he was here and in the years after he graduated. And then came 2004, when then 32-year-old Brian O'Connor took the team to a 44-15 record in his first year as its coach, winning ACC coach of the year in the process. Hugh Evans' point: "Who says a single person can't make a difference?" O'Connor has led the Cavaliers to eight consecutive NCAA tournaments, including the College World Series in 2009 when he earned two national coach of the year awards. Coach O'Connor and Coach Starsia believe in the importance of academic excellence. They also believe that good academics help us recruit better: but to believe that, it helps to know what it means to be a good student.

I taught political science at Northwestern for 12 years. One of my fondest memories was teaching "Introduction to World Politics" to Pat Fitzgerald, now Northwestern's

36-year-old head football coach, who recently signed another contract extension, this time for 10 years. Back then, Pat was an All-American linebacker for the Wildcats. He had broken his leg late in the 1995 season when Northwestern went to the Rose Bowl for the first time since 1949—losing to USC, in part because Pat couldn't play. He showed up for class on crutches, never late, and never missed a class. I only knew him as this handsome kid who always sat smack in the middle of the large lecture hall, and always (and mercifully) laughed at my jokes. When I passed out final papers, I called out his name and he came hobbling forward. I thought his name was vaguely familiar. So I said, "Pat Fitzgerald: where have I heard that name before?" The class roared with laughter at the fact that I did not know one of the most decorated athletes in school history. All I knew was that he worked very hard in my class, and earned the "A" that he received.

119

With the advent of "big time" college sports, it is perhaps inevitable that athletic coaches are often paid so much more than professors or academic administrators. They are increasingly the public faces of their universities, symbolizing their values, for good or for ill. That's why it's a good thing that Northwestern has someone of Pat Fitzgerald's intelligence and integrity, and that U.Va. has Dom Starsia, Brian O'Connor, Tony Bennett, Mike London and any number of very fine coaches of our 25 athletic teams. Last year, for the 24th time since the Academic-Achievement Award was instituted in 1981, U.Va. was again recognized for its football graduation rates; the team won the national award in 1985 and 1986. Virginia is one of just 12 programs to win this prestigious award and one of only six to win it twice.

No one at Virginia can excel both in the classroom and on the field without stringent discipline, close attention to time management, the talent that we seek to find and bring to Charlottesville from across the country and around the world, and perhaps most importantly, the burning desire to do your best, and be your best, at whatever you do.

In an earlier post, I referred to the brilliant symmetry of the baseball field, the uncanny distances between the mound and home plate or between the bases that perfectly match and test the athletic ability of human beings. On a lovely day last Friday (June 3), I sat at Davenport Field, amid a large crowd, watching Will Roberts retire one Navy Midshipman after another. He pitched a shutout, while striking out 14 and walking none. Will got all the support he needed from teammate Danny Hultzen, who went 3-for-4 with three RBIs. On Saturday night, Danny pitched U.Va. to a 10-2 win over St. John's in the second game of the regionals. Tyler Wilson gave Virginia its third straight stellar outing by a starting pitcher in a 13-1 win over East Carolina on Sunday. On Monday night, Danny was selected by the Seattle Mariners with the second overall pick in the Major League Baseball First-Year Player Draft—the highest draft selection in U.Va. baseball history. Will, Tyler and three other Virginia players—John Hicks, Steven Proscia and Kenny Swab—were chosen in rounds two through 30 of the draft on Tuesday.

In March, Will threw a perfect game against George Washington, only the second time it's happened in ACC history. It's only happened eight times in NCAA Division I baseball since 1957. Watching Will, Danny and Tyler pitch reminds us of the kind of excellence that is rarely attained in sports or other human endeavors. How hard is it to throw a baseball from 60 feet, six inches at over 90 miles an hour, and not allow a single batter to reach base over nine innings? How tough do you have to be to play lacrosse in 120-degree heat? Better still, how hard was it for our men's and women's cross country teams to go to the 2010 NCAA championships last fall while maintaining a 3.0 or better cumulative GPA? It seems that our student-athletes are striving for "perfect games" all the time.

This weekend, we will all follow the Cavaliers in the NCAA baseball tournament. Coach O'Connor said in an interview in March that at Virginia, "We're not one of those programs that have gotten to Omaha (site of the College World Series) year in and out. So that allows us to still have a feeling that we're still proving ourselves. It keeps an edge. I kind of like it." So do I, and I hope we go to Omaha this year. I know I'll be there—rooting for perfection.

REMEMBERING EDWARD KENNEDY, VIRGINIAN

THE UNIVERSITY OF VIRGINIA witnessed the passing of another great Virginian—a Virginian in the sense of his association with the University—just shy of two centuries, or 183 years to be precise, after the passing of the founder of the University. Ted Kennedy's ties to Virginia, of course, do not compare to those of Mr. Jefferson. Yet they are, in a sense, two bookends on the long and growing bookshelf that is the University, with the architect at the beginning and a man emblematic of an important moment in the University's history further down the shelf.

The two men were alike in ways that are profoundly revealing about our country. Both were aristocrats in a country that shunned aristocracy. Both were dominant figures in the Democratic Party. Both stood for the common man in spite of their great privilege, something reflective of the egalitarian aspirations of the country they loved. Both led large and complex families, in Kennedy's case, a legacy of three older brothers who died violent deaths while serving their country. Jefferson and Kennedy were patricians, patriots, and patriarchs.

Yet in spite of their privilege they were also "levelers," dedicating themselves to providing opportunities to those who lacked their inheritance. Jefferson was a slaveholder, of course, from a different era in our history; Kennedy was born to great wealth in a house full of servants, yet he was at the forefront of the civil rights movements that finally brought equality under the law to former slaves a century after the Civil War. And as both men grew older, they grew bolder, more outraged by inequality, yet with gravitas and dignity. They became more human, and humanized, at the end of their lives.

They were also alike in being bundles of contradictions. Jefferson had a long relationship with Sally Hemings, a beautiful black woman who was a half sister-in-law and, of course, a slave. Ted Kennedy long had a reputation as a womanizer. It took an appalling tragedy at Chappaquiddick for him to

123

become the most important champion of women's rights in the Senate. He also became, like Jefferson, a workaholic who was responsible for a myriad of legislation. (In the vast commentary after his death, his work on civil rights, voting rights, health care, immigration, the environment and many other endeavors were mentioned, but hardly anyone noted his long and sterling record as a champion for the rights of women.)

Ted Kennedy and the founder of our University were, in short, complicated men who lived and wrestled with their contradictions, both privately and in the public arena, always willing to fight the good fight, never downcast, and in the end better men for having confronted and tried to overcome their human-all-too-human frailties—even as their lives ended with battles still to be won.

When people say the United States is "the last, best hope of mankind" I often pause, because so many countries around the world have high standards of democracy and human rights. But there is something intangible about the United States, with its extraordinary complexity and diversity, part of a great continent anchored at the beginning by states as different as Massachusetts and Virginia, states that so embody that diversity— one, a former member of the Confederacy; the other, the most liberal state in our time; both, sites of the country's creation at Plymouth colony and Jamestown, and both producing great politicians who gave their all to overcome the worst legacies of our national heritage. And two great universities distinguish those states, Harvard, as one of the greatest private schools, and Virginia, as one of the greatest public schools, both overflowing with a diversity that would warm the capacious hearts of two great men, one the son of the Commonwealth of Virginia; the other, son of the Commonwealth of Massachusetts. One attended William and Mary and then went on to found the University of Virginia. The other attended Harvard and then had the good sense to come to Charlottesville to study the law. He would go on to become one of the great American lawmakers of the twentieth century.

At the University of Virginia we mourn the passing of an era, and of a formidable alumnus: we will miss Ted Kennedy.

125

MR. WILSON'S UNIVERSITY

THUMBING THROUGH A RECENT issue of the *Chronicle of Higher Education*, I came across an article entitled "Mr. Wilson's University." It discussed a conference held at Princeton that assessed the educational legacy of Woodrow Wilson, who had spent twenty years at Princeton, the last eight (1902-1910) as its president. In the article, John Milton Cooper Jr., the author of a recent biography of Woodrow Wilson, describes Princeton's relationship with Wilson as "ambivalent," going on to assert that Princeton had managed to avoid "filiopietism, in contrast to 'Mr. Jefferson's University,'" looking forward and not back. As an unreconstructed filiopietist, my curiosity was piqued.

The article contended that Wilson's educational legacy has been largely discredited, citing one historian after another who castigate Wilson for his shortcomings—his opposition to coeducation ("demoralizing dangers," he warned), his derision of the suffragettes (despite of his own daughters' activism), and his policy upholding the exclusion of African-Americans—all in an effort to keep Princeton compact and homogenous, a kind of WASP preserve where diversity, *avant la lettre*, encompassed the entire spectrum from E (Episcopal) to P (Presbyterian).

I suppose Wilson's record on race and civil liberties will always remain the battered kettle at his heel, with its clatter amplified by the present-ism of some in the academic profession. To point out that prejudice held sway throughout American society at the time, and that "scientific racism" was promulgated by some scientists at the best universities, does not excuse Wilson from his transgressions. But it would be most unfortunate if all this obscured his legacy as educator and statesman—and not just because Woodrow Wilson's influence on the modern university was an important one; the democratic principles and progressivism of his later life cannot be understood apart from his experience as an educator.

Wilson was a Virginian, born in nearby Staunton—where he would make his triumphant return after the 1912 election.

127

Although he did not betray much hint of a southern accent, he was at home in the South, the only place he said he understood thoroughly and instinctively. After Princeton he studied law at the University of Virginia, where he said he encountered intellectual rigor (as he wrote in a letter to a friend, "study is made a serious business and the loafer is an exception"). The teaching was better than any he had encountered before, "and the place is cosmopolitan," he explained, "at least as far as the South is concerned . . . and one feels that the intellectual forces of the South are forming here."

The University of Virginia had somehow survived without a president since its founding in 1819, when in 1898 it offered Wilson its first presidency. Graciously acknowledging that this may be the highest honor in his life, he nonetheless turned the offer down in favor of higher remuneration at Princeton—and eventually, its presidency. Had he accepted the offer it is possible that Virginia would have been, in addition to being Mr. Jefferson's University, Mr. Wilson's as well. (Instead we have one department in the College that bears his name: the Woodrow Wilson Department of Politics.)

Wilson's influence on the modern research university is woefully underappreciated—perhaps because most major initiatives for which he fought tooth and nail came to naught by the time he threw up his hands and left Princeton. Among them were his attempt to create a law school at Princeton like the one he knew at Virginia; his epic battle to disestablish Princeton's eating clubs; and his desire to place the

Graduate College at the center of the university as testament to Princeton's commitment to intellectual life.

In reality educational "Wilsonianism" presaged the modern research university, and embodied the characteristics of the modern professoriate. Wilson studied law, true, but he also had a Ph.D. in History and Political Science, and he worked his way up the academic ladder through his publications, climbing from Bryn Mawr, to Wesleyan and then to Princeton, improving his financial standing as well along the way. He was the first president at Princeton to have a Ph.D. (and the last American president to possess one), and one of the few university presidents who was a true academic superstar, presiding at the apex of his disciplinary field—a rarity then as it is now. Even at a university with a preponderance of undergraduates, he understood the critical role that graduate students could play in the intellectual life of the university. There were a number of fledgling "research universities" at the time—Chicago, Stanford, Cornell, and Hopkins—but no one could argue the case for the seamless integration of undergraduates and graduates quite as forcefully and persistently as Woodrow Wilson.

On the role of the university in a democracy, Mr. Wilson was more circumspect than the object of our filial piety, Mr. Jefferson. Our founder believed in a naturally occurring aristocracy of talent and virtue, liberally scattered across all segments of population—including the poor and the uneducated—and that it was the role of the university to "cull from

129

every condition of our people" this natural aristocracy and provide it with opportunity in the form of education. Wilson's conception, on the other hand, was more patrician than democratic, emphasizing the cultivation of an elite in service of the nation—"the minority who plan, who conceive, who superintend"—an elitism more European than American. Still: at Princeton Wilson fought to level social differences, made more insurmountable by the exclusive eating clubs. In the end, the eating clubs triumphed, his ignominious defeat driving him from academic life. But this marked the birth of a progressive statesman and one of the greatest legislative presidents in history—one who became even more fervent and eloquent in inveighing against social hierarchy at home, and the hierarchy of nations abroad.

130

Unlike Jefferson who devoted himself to creating the University after a long and illustrious political career, Wilson was a university educator before he entered national politics. For most of his adult life, Jefferson fought for democracy, and in retirement he sought to create in the University a lasting institution that would excavate and refine talent, the fruit of the nation he had worked so hard to build. By contrast, most of Wilson's adult life was spent in the university, and it was the experience of being at loggerheads with the Princeton's rich and powerful trustees and eating-club alumni that made him a crusader against the privileged, informing a view of democracy that he later came to espouse as president.

Woodrow Wilson imagined himself a Hamiltonian, seeing

government not as an intrusive entity but an organic embodiment of society, but as he grew older he became increasingly Jeffersonian, sharing with him the same optimism about human nature and the same belief in the university's role in creating equality and opportunities for all. Had he lived longer and retired to Old Nassau, his views on the role and the uses of the university might not have veered far from the ones he learned in Charlottesville. Since his time there, Princeton overcame the elitism and privilege of that century-old era, to become not just a great university dedicated to scholarly excellence, but one of extraordinary diversity. Mr. Wilson would have been proud.

131

IN LOCO PARENTIS

LAST WEEK, AS THE Class of 2010 prepared to graduate and join the ranks of some one hundred thousand alumni of the College, they received a letter from me that adumbrated an aspect of their new life that our alumni know all too well: I asked them to consider making a gift to the College. There would be no amount too small, for the point of the fourth-year gift is in the act of giving itself, a rite of passage marking an exchange of roles between student and teacher. As students, they were supported by their teachers, receiving instruction and advice that will direct the course of their lives. As alumni, they become the patrons of their teachers, providing the opportunity for others to receive the same education, while offering support and counsel to their teachers. I offered to match a portion of their giving from my own funds under a program the students call "Make the Dean Pay"; if more than 2,010 members of the Class of 2010 (which numbers 2,968) participated, I promised to commit more.

Shortly after sending out the message, I received a thoughtful response from a member of the Class of 2010, who argued that the burden on his family of paying four years of out-of-state tuition has been arduous—and even under-appreciated, given that out-of-state students can be seen as de facto subsidizers of our in-state and AccessUVA students. In light of that, the call to give yet more money struck him as excessive.

I understood his point. His class is staring at a troubled labor market, with the jobless rate holding steady at 9.6 percent, and 36,000 jobs disappearing in February. If there are signs that we may be out of the Great Recession, they are not strong enough to signal that we are on the way to a recovery. Meanwhile, the rate of underemployment is creeping upward, as more people cut hours for lack of full-time jobs.

The Greek goddess of wisdom, Athena, famously leapt full-blown from the brow of Zeus. We sometimes think of the University as Athena, arising spontaneously from the mind of Mr. Jefferson, and then living at the Olympian heights, unsullied by the troubles of the world. Athena emerged clad in

133

divine armor. But the University has never had such protection, always subject—and now more than ever—to the vicissitudes of the state and national economies.

We are a public University, committed to the highest standards of education for all students, in-state and out-of-state. Yet public resources have never been enough to accomplish that mission alone, and the gap between resources and needs has never been greater. However onerous out-of-state tuition may be for many, it still does not pay for the cost of an education; the rest comes from philanthropic gifts and proceeds from endowments supporting research and scholarships of all kinds. In other words, the College is not a money-making institution but a money-losing institution; we subsidize not just in-state students but out-of-state students as well.

134

The economic downturn that has devastated so many of the families of our students has also struck the College, hard. And during the downturn, the College has remained strongly mindful of the sacrifices that parents make to send their children to Virginia. We have worked hard to keep our tuition below that of our peer institutions, both private and public. As a result, the College has to depend on alumni giving more than ever.

The first responsibility of our students after their graduation is to their parents, who in many cases sacrificed so much to allow their children to receive the best education in the world, an education that will launch them into life and career. But our fourth-year students joined a second family when they walked onto the Lawn in the fall of 2006, the family of the University of Virginia. And like their birth families, they will remain members of that family for as long as they live.

There was once much debate about whether colleges and universities served *in loco parentis*, a Latin phrase that means "in the place of the parents." The question was the extent to which universities could and should regulate the social and political activities of its students; the consensus was that the powers of the university are limited in these domains. But in a larger sense, some of the best things about the parent-child relationship exist between alma mater (which does mean "nourishing mother," after all) and student. The gifts of the natal parent to the child can never be repaid. The gifts of the alma mater are different, but no less real. The fourth-year gift is a rite of passage, and like most rites, it is rich in meaning, both symbolic and real.

135

III

ARISTOCRACY
of
TALENT

E PLURIBUS UNUM: AN ADDRESS TO A JEFFERSONIAN CLASS

138

I AM HONORED to be with you, who have so distinguished yourselves in your studies, and with your families and friends, who take great pride in your accomplishments. Your class is of particular meaning to me. I am mindful that you are more or less twenty years old, born around 1989. I have a son born in 1989, that remarkable year in world politics, and so I have many reasons for having thought hard about the coming of age of people like yourselves, and the world that has shaped you. One might say that you are a privileged generation—the first class ever to have been born and reared in a world that was spared the agonies of what the historian Eric Hobsbawm has called the Age of Extremes, which he dates from World War I and the Bolshevik Revolution and that ended with the Fall of the Berlin Wall. For him, this period frames what was the essence of the 20th century—extremes of war, communism, fascism, racism, the Holocaust, and mass exterminations.

However terrible our recent problems–ethnic cleansing in the former Yugoslavia, 9/11, the brutalities of terrorism and the antediluvian Taliban wanting to rule Afghanistan and maybe the modern world as well—those events do not compare with the large scale brutalities of organized madness of the twentieth century. I remember holding my infant son, who seemed like a bundle of undifferentiated protoplasm, while watching students spill out into Tiananmen Square in Beijing, and in the autumn the Fall of Berlin Wall, as young people smashed it with sledgehammers. I was riveted to the television, in awe of the world that was crumbling before our very eyes and full of trepidations for the world to come. My son was named Ian—Scottish for John, but in Chinese Korean script, it means "doubly peaceful," reflecting the hopes that 1989, the year of your birth, spawned.

We are also aware of another significant 20th anniversary: the unusually long tenure of our president John Casteen at the time of his retirement next year—a great president who has an encyclopedic memory of the events of his tenure and

139

a remarkable understanding of the recondite and complex nature of the University. By virtue of his tenure as president coinciding with your lifetime so far, he is also a president spared the extremes of ideological prisms through which scholars peered at the world; like you, his presidency was born into a world happier, more prosperous and tolerant, more forgiving of differences.

Gertrude Stein, in her book on Picasso, once defined the artistic spirit as one that is effortlessly contemporary, one that intuits and acts upon the zeitgeist. Not surprisingly, throughout his presidency John Casteen has advocated and exemplified the best virtues of internationalization that the post-1989 era portended, and he tried his best to infuse them into the University of Virginia, a university that truly cares about history and learns from it.

I myself came to America as a foreign student, guided by no more vision and sense of assurance than a picture I'd seen in National Geographic: a photo of a house shuttered for the winter in snowbound, forested Maine, which suggested a heart-breaking, desolate beauty, that was reminiscent of my ancestral home surrounded by mountains on the east coast of Korea. Clutching my National Geographic, I arrived at Kennedy airport in the middle of the night, took a cab to Port Authority Terminal and boarded a Greyhound bus for Maine. That was thirty three years ago; now I find myself at Mr. Jefferson's University, as dean no less. In *Facing West*, one of my favorite poems in Walt Whitman's *Leaves of Grass*, he writes:

140

For, starting westward from Hindustan, from the vales of Kashmere

From Asia—from the north—from the God, the sage, and the hero

From the south—from the flowery peninsulas, and the spice islands

Long having wander'd since—round the earth having wander'd

Now I face home again—very pleas'd and joyous.

The notion that the University of Virginia has become home for this dean who started so far away may strike you as quixotic, until you remember that Thomas Jefferson was the most cosmopolitan and worldly president we have ever had, and the first faculty members he recruited to teach local youth were mostly foreigners—a thought that was anathema to many Virginians of the time. Franklin Delano Roosevelt was also cosmopolitan, also patrician, like his cousin Teddy, but they had nothing on Mr. Jefferson. Not just because he was Ambassador to France; or because he knew seven languages; or because he so widely traveled, replicating the visual splendor of Italy on the Lawn. But because he instinctively understood and insisted that what was uniquely American could be also uniquely and ingeniously worldly, that America could be coterminous with the world, without the conquering ambitions so often associated with such wishes.

To realize his complex vision of America both pastoral and worldly, innocent and learned, he wanted to create a university different from nearly all American colleges—the Harvards, Yales, and the Princetons, founded during the colonial period, and over three dozen more colleges that sprouted up in the

141

early days of the federal union, which were mostly established by religious denominations as you know. He wanted something fitted to the distinctive American experience. Thus, the University was conceived as a profoundly American, and, cosmopolitan place: civilized, learned, open-minded, un-parochial. If in the first days of the University, the actions of some local hoodlums broke his heart, that still does not diminish the fact that his cosmopolitanism is truly your birthright.

I mentioned earlier that you are a class unscathed by the Age of Extremes, and in this you are the perfect class to embody the dreams of Mr. Jefferson—he fought in an anti-colonial revolution that was, compared to many others, not so bloody; he died before the bloodiest American conflict, the Civil War. He was a classic idealist in the American grain, and in the best sense of idealism tempered by historical experience.

You are also one of the most diverse classes to arrive at the university. Look at yourselves: you are diverse, measured by the usual metrics—by ethnicity, race, and nationality—much of it owing to that universe unto itself known as Northern Virginia. In Northern Virginia it is said that there are over one hundred languages and dialects spoken—and it is teeming with Arab-Americans, Afghan-Americans, Korean-Americans, Indian-Americans, Salvadorans, Peruvians, Colombians, and the Bolivians—the largest such community in the US resides in Arlington. There is also a sizable African population—Nigerians, Kenyans, Ethiopians. They are enriching our community, and we are responding.

In the College of Arts and Sciences alone, we teach 26 languages from Spanish to Yiddish, Urdu, Sanskrit, Bengali, Swahili and also sign language. With students from 148 countries, you are a veritable United Nations, distinguished not by how you look, but who you have become: excellent in what you do. The Commonwealth of Virginia is not just diverse, but excellent because the heritage of the original settlers (whom we think we see over at Williamsburg) commingles with the dynamism of the immigrants who bring their own outlooks and skills. Here in this great state, tradition and innovation go hand in hand, a great bellwether for the future of the nation.

You are diverse by another measure of diversity: excellence. Let me advance this proposition: diversity is excellence, and we shall measure our excellence by the way we cherish and work with differences.

I had a colleague at the University of Michigan, Scott Page, a game theorist who wrote a very fine book called *The Difference*. It is full of equations that show groups that display a range of perspectives outperform groups of like-minded experts. Diversity yields superior outcomes, and difference beats out homogeneity, whether you're talking about citizens in a democracy or scientists in the laboratory. The best collective whole that exceeds the sum of its parts is one that relies on human diversity—not what we look like from outside, but what we look like from within, our distinct tools and abilities.

The world faces enormously complex problems that require truly creative solutions. To solve those problems, we need people with diverse skills—people with different ways of conceptualizing, imagining, and doing things; people with different life experiences and different memories of what worked and what didn't; people with different referents. People who think alike, with the same referents, experiences, and skill sets cannot get quite as far in solving complex problems. That's why Silicon Valley, with the variegated multitude of humanity from every background, revolutionized the world and continues to go forward from strength to strength; why Manhattan, a magnet for humanity from everywhere, is so dynamic, constantly reinventing capitalism as it resuscitates and rejuvenates it.

Diversity has its pitfalls, too, as we know; but when well led and disciplined, it leads to a curious kind of homogeneity. Let's think about baseball, since we are in the high season of American baseball, with the "World Series" around the corner. It used to be a joke—a "world series" in America—but now it isn't, because the players come from everywhere. The other day I was watching a replay of the Olympic gold medal baseball game between Cuba and Korea, when the Koreans made a double play with the bases loaded. After a while, I rubbed my eyes to realize I was having some difficulty telling who was Cuban and who was Korean, they all looked the same because they moved the same; the way they stretch before they hit; the way they chew gum; the way they play their positions; the body language of the shortstop and second baseman as they execute a double play; the way they give each other high fives;

the way they pat each other on the butt; the way they glare at the umpire, protesting in whatever language but the same the world over. They are all just players—they have the same body language, same plays, and same rules.

Baseball cannot exist without rules—the baseball rule of law: the pitcher stands sixty feet six inches away, the bases are 90 feet apart. Change either measure, and it is a different game. If Nolan Ryan had stood 50 feet away with his fireball, no one could have hit him. Take five feet away from the basepaths, and anyone can steal a base—but at 90 feet, only the fastest players can do so. It's amazing how well these old, 19th-century rules have worked to make the game so challenging and so exciting. It is said that there is no action in all of sports more difficult than hitting a major league pitch.

The rules require everyone to conform to them, as chess does, and out of that comes a beautiful human choreography on the baseball field. You do things, you excel, and at the moment of excellence and accomplishment, as you do, you begin to look alike in your excellence as distinguished people, and that is something wonderful. It isn't an accident, because if you excel in math or physics or art or history, you cross home plate with an A regardless of who you are or what you look like. That's why the Cubans and the Koreans in the Gold medal game merged seamlessly into one mold: baseball player. You will merge into physicist, scholar, lawyer, doctor—and maybe a player in the pros.

For diversity and difference to thrive and translate into

excellence, there has to be hard work, discipline, conformity to rules and respect for community.

Perhaps we are entering into the twilight of diversity, in the sense that we have so rightly stressed diversity for decades now, and have achieved so much. Yet the great universities can now be melting pots, creating people with common pools of knowledge in different fields, who know and play by the rules, and distinguish themselves by merit—just as Jackie Robinson's speed was perfect for racing 90 feet and sliding safely home. In this sense I would hope that you would all look the same and act the same, in your chosen fields—to excel as learned historians, or biologists, or engineers. Here is something that is indeed singular in your achievements: you are inquisitive, humane, and worldly—educated citizens in Jefferson's best sense.

And since you are the first class to have lived outside the Age of Extremes, your citizenly duty is to make sure those extremes remain an unfortunate part of the past. Yours is an open age, to learn, experiment, find out what works for you. It is an optimistic age, in spite of our economic difficulties. It is a Jeffersonian age, because all things worldly are open to you. Do your best to try and meet his standards—very high ones, but in the end, Mr. Jefferson's standards are also signs of a life well lived.

THE
DESEGREGATED
HEART

ON THE OCCASION marking the birth of Martin Luther King Jr., we might pause to reflect on the early days of integration at the University of Virginia, going back now six decades. It was in 1950 that Gregory Swanson, a black attorney from Danville, successfully sued to gain admission to the Law School. For years, African-American scholars had been seeking admission to the graduate program, going all the way back to 1935, when Alice Jackson of Richmond applied to the graduate school in French. She was sent away, as others later would also be, accompanied by a state scholarship to study at a northern university of her choice (in this case, Columbia University). But Gregory Swanson took a different tack, and actually enrolled at the University, if only for a brief period. One of the changes he made occurred to the mind and heart of Sarah Patton Boyle, social activist and author of The Desegregated Heart, published in 1962.

Boyle was married to a faculty member in the Drama Department in the College. A descendant of southern aristocracy, she writes in her memoir that she was taught to think of herself "as a part of the very backbone of Virginia, which was the backbone of the South, which was the backbone of nation, which was the backbone of the world." For her, the University of Virginia was simply the University, as it was for so many, and she spoke of the University with a pride that was nearly proprietary. The prospect of racial integration at the University, heralded by the impending admission of Gregory Swanson, was a deadly serious matter, commanding her focus so urgently and singularly that all else would be swept aside. In the course of confronting it, she was transformed, as her beloved Virginia—both the state and university—would be.

In the Virginia Spectator, she responded to the question of why she believed in integration: "I believe in integration because of what you might characterize as 'wild idealism.' I don't wince at admitting this because it is with wild idealism that all human progress is made." But her "wild idealism" was always infused with a kind of level-headedness. Although she was not trained as a social scientist, she had the habit of a sociologist committed to getting the facts right—before she proceeded to upset the apple cart.

The first thing she examined was her own heart—and the implicit assumptions about race that resided there. Through her correspondence with Gregory Swanson, and her numerous faux pas in encounters with him, she tried to understand the source of the patronizing paternalism that lay just below the surface of her liberalism. When she heard from the editor of The Tribune, the local black newspaper in Charlottesville, that he had little patience with "the gross paternalism of the 'Master class'-turned-liberal," she even set up a tutorial with him to educate herself about the mind of black folks, seeking to recast the contours of her heart. Her stories are poignant, as when she describes being shocked the first time she heard a black person call himself a "Southerner" (rather than a "Southern Negro"); or, writing what she thought was a great essay about why "We Want a Negro at the UVa" (because for "all his assurance and courage [Swanson] has not a trace of defiance," and "he has a sure sense of where rights cease and privileges begin"). She was utterly baffled when Swanson reacted coolly, rather than gratefully, to her essay.

But remake her heart she did, and she proceeded to publish a remarkable number of articles and columns in newspapers in the Commonwealth, providing her readers with statistics under the heading of "Facts and Figures of Good

Will," as well as the questions and answers about race relations that always began with the following message in Italics: "Segregation is America's iron curtain. Its greatest evil has been that it prevents us from understanding each other and from being conscious of each other's growth. On both sides of the curtain we are about fifty years behind in our interpretation of the other. Write in questions concerning racial attitudes of the educated white Southerner of today. (Names will be withheld)."

In 1955 she also wrote a piece for the Saturday Evening Post, entitled "We Are Readier than We Think." It was re-titled by the editors, without her consent, as "Southerners Will Like Integration," earning her the lasting enmity of many of her fellow southerners and a burning cross in her front yard. If the timing of the piece was flawed (it appeared shortly before the Massive Resistance against public school integration), her logic was not. She argued that the South was ready for integration, as evidenced by a 1948 poll of the faculty in the South, including at the University of Virginia, showing that 69 percent of the respondents favored integration at the level of graduate and professional education; at the University of Virginia, some 79 percent of those polled were said to be in favor. A 1950 random poll of University of Virginia graduate students also reported that 73 percent of the returned ballots (216 in total) checked "No Objection" to having black students in class. Why then was there a gap in perception, with people assuming that there was insurmountable resistance to integration? Her answer was cultural: she argued that a conviction prevailed in the South that "everybody else is prejudiced." The constant fear of "trouble" hid the reality of significant support for integration.

After Brown vs. the Board of Education in 1954 she appeared before the Public Education Hearing for the Commonwealth. She stayed on message: "Many Southerners like myself actually would prefer integrated schools. Change is something we often need but seldom care for, and most of us will applaud those who give us excuses to avoid the many efforts involved in change .... There is nothing in our hearts to make this change difficult if only we get a little help from our leaders. The silent majority of our people are able, and under proper leadership would be willing, to meet democratic and Christian ideals."

Today is a day to contemplate the words of this remarkable Virginian. It is also a day to pause to consider what has, and has not, been achieved since they were written fifty-six years ago.

AT TACKLE, CHESTER PIERCE

THE LAST POST of my blog, tracing the early days of racial integration on Grounds ("The Desegregrated Heart"), sparked a number of fascinating recollections and discussions from our alumni. One was an exchange between two Psychology majors—Tom Pettigrew '52 and Brawner Cates '67—about the first integrated football team to play south of the Mason-Dixon Line, Scott Stadium, 1947. On April 15 of that year, Jackie Robinson played first base for the Brooklyn Dodgers against the Boston Braves. On October 11, Chester

Pierce, an African-American, played tackle for Harvard against Virginia. It was the practice at that time for integrated college teams to leave their black players at home when they played in the South.

The trip to Virginia was not a pleasant one for Pierce. He was not allowed to stay in the same hotel with his white teammates; his pain was not assuaged when the University housed him in a nearby mansion. When he came to the team hotel for meals, he was not allowed to enter through the front door. In a show of solidarity, his teammates also entered through the kitchen. The night before the game, President Colgate W. Darden spoke at a pep rally attended by about 3,000: "Chester Pierce, a Negro, is a guest of the University of Virginia, and nothing would shame us more than having an unfortunate incident during the game." And nothing untoward took place—except to Harvard: it lost to Virginia, 47-0. But history was made, and Pierce became the first black man to play football in the South against a white team—and later, the first to play lacrosse against Maryland and Navy. Like Jim Brown, Pierce excelled at both football and lacrosse.

But unlike Jim Brown, he did not go into the NFL. Instead, Chet Pierce went on to become one of the most influential psychiatrists of our time. After Harvard College and Harvard Medical School, he served on three faculties there: Psychiatry, Public Health, and Education. His research examined the impact of extreme environments and racism on human psychology. He also wrote on sports medicine and the effect of the media on blacks and children. He was elected president of the American Board of Psychiatry and Neurology.

Pierce never talked much about the 1947 Virginia game, or for that matter, about his role in integrating collegiate sports. "I never talk about that," he told a Crimson reporter, standing not far from Mass General, which today houses the Pierce Global Psychiatry Division, "I didn't do anything." He said in another interview that it was mere chance that he was a participant in that historic moment at Virginia; he was practically a bystander, he said, just watching things unfold before his eyes.

Chet Pierce's absence of triumphalism reflects his profound insight into the catastrophic problem of racism at all levels in our society. He showed how racism operates on both the macro (political and institutional) level and the micro level. He labeled the everyday insults that black people suffer "micro-aggressions," which he defined as the "subtle, stunning, often automatic, and non-verbal exchanges which are 'put-downs' of the blacks by offenders." These put-downs, seemingly innocent, could slowly crush the human spirit under a devastating burden, leading to a lack of self-esteem and confidence, and eventually to shorter lives.

In the South, he saw de jure racism; in the North he saw de facto racism. He was careful to distinguish between these two distinct forms of racism, condoning neither. But he did see the de jure racism of the South as an institution in the throes of death, whether or not he had participated in its demise at Scott Stadium. Later in his life, he wrote that "one

154

must not look for the gross and obvious. The subtle, cumulative mini-assault is the substance of today's racism."

As an undergraduate at Harvard, Pierce never felt completely accepted. He had white roommates who were members of private clubs; the question of his becoming a member somehow never came up. In retrospect, he said, he regretted never being invited to join the Hasty Pudding Club—the one membership he thought he fully deserved, given his facility with composition, piano, accordion, and trumpet. Still, he continued to have great respect for institutions like Harvard and even Hasty Pudding, always taking pains to explain the distinction between whites acting as individuals versus as members of a dominant collective. It was also a way for him to protect himself, and not be disappointed by the unthinking racism of his fellow students. He remained vigilant against people who, even unknowingly, wreaked psychological havoc on minorities, keeping a record of these incidents—from the behavior of the bar owner in Cambridge who refused to let him in, to a professor at High Table in Lowell House who called out to him: "You, black man, where do you come from?"

Sixty three years after Chet Pierce played in the first racially integrated football game at Virginia, much has changed—for the better, and for the worse. The South has long since integrated, with the racial demography of the students at the University of Virginia looking not much different than that at Harvard. But if de jure racism is a thing of past, de facto racism is not—just as Pierce feared. Micro-aggressions still confront every black person, but there are new macro trends that are also disturbing.

Vesla Weaver, Assistant Professor in Politics in the College, writes in an important book, Frontlash: Civil Rights, the Carceral State, and the Transformation of American Politics, that the era of Civil Rights coincides with a massive expansion of the American criminal justice system. In 1965 there were 780,000 adults under correctional authority of any type; by 2008, that population had exploded to seven million, more than the entire population of Virginia. The black rate of incarceration increased at an even faster rate—four times the increase of whites. In 1974 2.2 percent of white males, 13.4 percent of black males, and 4.0 percent of Hispanic males could expect to go to prison during their lifetime. Today 33 percent of black men over 18 are under some type of criminal supervision. In her second book Professor Weaver argues that it is no longer simply a harsh social environment that leads to greater incarceration of black people, but, increasingly the other way round: the high rates of incarceration have huge negative impacts on the political incorporation and inequality of black families and neighborhoods.

In his work, Chet Pierce was interested in extreme environments—both physical and psychological. He argued that, for psychological and physiological adjustment, it was much more difficult to be a ten-year old inhabitant of Harlem than to be a forty-year old astronaut in outer space; there was simply not enough societal support for that youngster in

Harlem. He often observed that whites in power fail to consider the impact that their decisions have on black people, arguing that it was essential for black intellectuals to focus on black interests with clarity and sustained commitment—something he did all his life.

P.S.: That Harvard-Virginia game was a home game in more ways than one. Pierce's father was from Portsmouth.

157

"VIRGINIA" AT FORTY

" **BUT IF EVER** a girl looked as if she were cut out for happiness!" exclaimed an old school teacher when she caught sight of Virginia, the heroine of Ellen Glasgow's novel of the same name, set in a southern town called Dinwiddie. In the story, Virginia wasn't ready for happiness: the virtues she had been taught—to be self-effacing, to make no demands, to put others before herself, to be bound by duty and honor—would prove a hindrance to the happiness that she had seemed destined for, given her good family and good looks.

"Virginia" is a tableau of a "southern lady," an idée fixe that was already fading when Glasgow's novel was published in 1913. She called the novel "a history of manners," one that sought to give meaning to "the South," as so many writers had done in the decades before.

In time, Virginia's world would crumble: Dinwiddie, loosely modeled on Petersburg, surrenders to industrialism; her children grow up and leave home—including daughters who go off to college, each with her own sense of purpose and person. Her husband, whose success and contentment provided her own, would desert her for another woman. The novel ends with her returning home after her husband breaks her heart. Standing on the porch, "she stopped and looked back into the street as she might have looked back at the door of a prison." For Virginia at forty, the past looked as bleak as the future.

Glasgow herself was an advocate of women's rights, taking part in marches for the right to vote in the first decade of the twentieth century. She went on to win the Pulitzer Prize for fiction and in 1931 she chaired the Southern Writers Conference, held on Grounds, a distinct honor for a woman writer, at a College that had no women.

The first classes of women in the College, some 450 first years and second- and third-year transfers, did not step onto the Lawn until September 1970, forty years ago. Those were turbulent times; the year before, four women had sued the University, represented by the American Civil Liberties

Union, and one ("Virginia" Scott, no less) enrolled in the fall of 1969. At the end of that academic year, on May 4, 1970, National Guard troops opened fire on students demonstrating against the Vietnam War, leaving four dead in Ohio. Marches and strikes erupted on campuses across the nation, including the one in Charlottesville. The first classes of undergraduates that included women began their studies just four months later. And as those women graduated from the College beginning in 1972, they entered a working world they coveted but had not anticipated—one of economic stagnation, high inflation and unemployment. But they held their own and they prospered. Meanwhile, their alma mater kept taking and educating more women; today women constitute 61 percent of the College population, greater than the university-wide average of 56 percent. This is remarkable, considering that it was the College that had been the last bulwark against co-education in the university (graduate and professional schools went co-ed in 1920).

Glasgow's character Virginia was what sociologists might call an "ideal type," an ideational construct that gives expression to the realities of a time and place by embodying certain characteristics, and in this case, of a real person—probably her own mother. On Grounds today, there are no ideal types of "the south," let alone "the southern lady," as defined in Glasgow's novel of manners. Women have come to Charlottesville from all over the world; to the extent that one senses "the south" in them, it is perhaps in their courteousness, part

160

of the ineffable culture that still permeates the College. But even when they hail from below the Mason-Dixon Line, our undergraduate women are unlikely to define themselves as "southern," any more than the College is defined by its region.

In February, Cheryl Mills ('87), the counselor and chief of staff to Hillary Clinton, gave a talk at a conference on women's leadership. An unassuming woman with an easy laugh, and an extraordinary intellect, she proceeded to regale the audience with a story that was as funny as it was revealing of the distance we have traveled. Cheryl worked her way through college and in her last year was co-chair of the resident staff program. During move-in, a mother of an incoming student found out that her daughter would have an African-American roommate; distressed, she sought out a resident advisor to ask about a reassignment. As luck would have it, the resident advisor was African-American. The mother asked to speak to her supervisor, the senior resident advisor, only to find that she too was African-American. Dismayed, she moved yet higher up the chain of command, which brought her to Cheryl, the co-chair of the resident staff program—who is African-American. Undeterred, she asked to meet a dean in charge of residence life program; without protest, Cheryl escorted her to the dean, and wouldn't you know it, she was also African-American.

By the time that Cheryl arrived on the Grounds from her native Baltimore in 1983, it was already a very different place from what even then was called "the Old South." But with

161

her unusual good humor and intelligence, she also helped to change it, making it both more interesting and more open. In her talk, she recounted the lessons learned from the College that have stayed with her. One was the important art of listening, and of building consensus; not being hierarchical but collegial; and above all, remaining always courteous. She also talked about the ethics of service, of being committed to a purpose larger than oneself. Listening to her speak, I thought to myself that it would be difficult to find a woman that embodies the spirit of the College more perfectly than Cheryl Mills.

Exactly what "our" Virginia has become after forty years of co-education is an interesting question. On a glorious spring day like today, our undergraduate women might be sitting on the Lawn, discussing Spanish literature in a seminar, their faces luminous like the star magnolias lurching toward them from across the pathway. It makes for a pretty picture, a pentimento of a "southern lady," still courteous and still committed to a cause larger than herself, but with a fundamentally different claim to her place in the world than the one that Glasgow's Virginia contemplated. Our Virginia is "cut out for happiness" indeed, but also cut out for ambition, accomplishment, and a new place in the sun.

THE "SCIENTIFIC CONSPIRACY OF NATIONS": VIRGINIA IN BERLIN

FIFTY YEARS AFTER David Bruce (College '20), one of the most distinguished diplomats of the 20th century, occupied the residence of the American embassy in Germany, another Virginian followed in his footsteps. Tammy Snyder Murphy (College '87) is married to the current U.S. Ambassador, Philip Murphy. To celebrate the College's budding relationship with Humboldt University, Ambassador and Mrs. Murphy hosted a dinner last month, bringing to their residence not just the delegations from Virginia and Humboldt but representatives of Germany's great foundations—the Max Planck Institute, the German Academic Exchange Service (DAAD), the Leibniz Society, and the Alexander Humboldt Foundation. If this sounds very formal, the Murphy children briefly left their homework to come down to join us, leavening the otherwise all too earnest academic discussion; that, combined with catching up on all the College news, gave a special intimacy to the celebratory dinner, as if it were a family affair.

Earlier in the day, the Ambassador and his wife had given me a tour of the new American embassy in Pariser Platz, along the famous boulevard Unter den Linden. It had been built in an open field that until 1990 had been left to fester by the East German regime, bearing mute witness to the spectacular ruins of German modernity. Today the vista from the embassy, opening out to the Brandenburg Gate and the Reichstag, bears witness to another kind of modernity. On the walls of the embassy upstairs are the names of the American envoys to Germany, from John Quincy Adams to Phil Murphy, and of the high commissioners of occupied Germany—men like John J. McCloy, whom John F. Kennedy once described as "the godfather of free Germany" for his contributions to the transition from Nazi Germany to West Germany.

The College has an ongoing relationship with Humboldt University through a research consortium on the study of "lifespan"—life's evolutionary and ontogenetic dynamics—a consortium that includes the Max Planck Institute and the

University of Michigan. Now we are exploring the possibilities for fusing Humboldt's scholarly talents with ours in a wide range of areas, including the history of literature and philosophy; religious studies; sociology; media studies; theatre; Jewish studies; and political theory.

The University of Virginia and Humboldt University have a somewhat similar provenance. They sprang into being roughly at the same time, from the minds of men who exemplified the best possibilities of their civilization. Wilhelm von Humboldt and his brother Alexander were remarkably similar to Thomas Jefferson in their intellectual orientations. All three believed in the infinite possibilities for the development of the human mind, and hence had an abiding concern with university education. This led Wilhelm von Humboldt to create a structure that combined both teaching and research in one institution—in other words, a research university, one that became the template in this country for Johns Hopkins, the University of Michigan, and the University of Chicago, among others. They also believed in the unity and interrelation of the sciences, based on evidence and not theology, measured with great fastidiousness using the latest technology—in other words, they were, *avant la lettre*, Humboldtian scientists.

Furthermore, the Humboldt brothers believed not just in the unity of the sciences but of scientists—and in the "scientific conspiracy of nations," connecting scholars from all over Europe—from Sweden, Prussia, France, England, Russia, Italy—and the United States. Alexander also mentored

165

scientists from Latin America, a rarity at the time. In fact, Alexander von Humboldt led expeditions of scientific exploration to South America, just as Jefferson sent Lewis and Clark across North America. One might say that Jefferson was Humboldtian and the Humboldt brothers were Jeffersonian. It is little wonder that Mr. Jefferson delighted in hosting Alexander at the White House, holding long conversations about the state of science as well as the results of Alexander's travels.

The "scientific conspiracy of nations" took a curious turn in the century that followed, to the near ruination of the German university, and inversely, the flourescence of the American. Humboldt University, which had been home to men whose work defined the apotheosis of western civilization in modern times—Fichte, Hegel, Schleiermacher, Schopenhauer, Schelling, Einstein, Max Planck, Marx, Engels, Heine, Bismarck, Liebknecht, only to name a few—in the immediate aftermath of Hitler's rise to power in 1933 expelled some two hundred fifteen Jewish professors and employees and rescinded numerous doctorates. This involuntary European scholarly diaspora led to the immigration of over 100 physicists to the United States, amounting to 25 percent of the pre-1933 physics community in Germany and nearly half of its theoretical physicists. Einstein was of course the most prominent; a few years after he came to the U.S. he was visited by an old friend and colleague. Einstein asked him, "How is German physics?" His response: "There is no German

166

physics." The stimulus given by refugee physicists to biology, as exemplified by the Watson-Crick model of the DNA molecule, or to nuclear physics for the Manhattan project, would not have been possible, save for this massive diaspora. As German universities became shells of their former selves, American research universities, opening their arms to the scholars fleeing Europe, were spreading their wings toward a golden age of scholarship.

Just as Pariser Platz is finally restored, re-populated by elegant buildings that speak to hope and to the future, so is Humboldt University, seemingly ready to reclaim the legacy of the Augustan age of the eighteen century, when the German states were world centers of culture, and in the nineteenth century when German science and technology flourished in a university system that was the best in the world, bar none. But is that really the past which is the prelude to the German future?

The pictures of men that hang in the American embassy point, just as easily, to a different past as prelude to the future: the sharp break in German history in 1945 and the relative longevity of the Federal Republic. During this time the United States tried its best to help create a new Germany, persuading it to turn around and look west, to work with France and integrate their iron and steel industries under the Schuman Plan, to anchor its economy deep in the European market, and to integrate the Bundeswehr into NATO operations. The important political actors—parties, the state bureaucracy, interest groups, the federal reserve, individual states, the supreme court, and the media—would become so closely tied to one another that changes, when they came, were only in small, incremental steps. Yet when the Berlin Wall suddenly fell in 1989, the U.S. quickly supported the major step of German reunification, over opposition from England and other allies. Almost as suddenly Humboldt University emerged from its East German shell and quickly began recouping its previous global stature.

So it seems today that the future of this great German university derives both from its Humboldtian past, but also shrewd postwar American policies and the continuing American presence in Bonn and now in Berlin: really a positive outcome by all measures. Two centuries after Alexander von Humboldt's visit with Thomas Jefferson, we might call it a truly Jeffersonian outcome.

168

THE QUEST FOR THE GOLDEN FLEECE

LAST WEEK I MADE a visit to Semester at Sea, a shipboard program which the University of Virginia sponsors. It is essentially a floating university that circumnavigates the globe, offering an experience akin to a string of study abroad programs. Nineteen students and four faculty from the University of Virginia are participating this semester, on a voyage that so far has taken them to the Bahamas, Dominica, the Brazilian Amazon, and Ghana; as I write, the ship should be hewing close to the west coast of Africa on its way down to Cape Town.

I met them in Takoradi, Ghana's first deep water seaport. It is a drab city of ramshackle huts, offering so little virtue and interest to visitors that Lonely Planet advises there is "no reason to stick around." But buried in this city, perched on what the British called the Gold Coast, is a lot of history. Much of it has to do with "globalization," which began more than five hundred years ago when the Portuguese came in search of gold—and then slaves. Since then, Ghana has been a harbinger for other kinds of globalization, some of it political and intellectual, others commercial. One conjures up three different types of globalization, layered into a kind of pentimento of modernity, revealing the inseparability of the past with the present. It is a complex layering, one that escapes comprehension through the linear imagination that for so long characterized ideas like progress, modernization, and development.

Ghana's early encounter with the West was disastrous. With the spread of plantations in the Americas in the sixteenth century, the slave trade eclipsed the traffic in gold, and Ghana became home to a number of slave trading centers. Near Takoradi are the scattered castles and forts that held in their "slave dungeons" the men and women sold or captured all over West Africa, including today's Benin, Niger, and Burkina Faso; and there they waited, hundreds of people forced into windowless, dank prisons for weeks and months, only to be shackled and chained and then loaded onto ships bound for the Americas—especially North America and the Caribbean. Until the slave trade was outlawed in the early nineteen century, it is estimated that twelve million Africans arrived in the New World, to provide labor in cotton and coffee plantations, gold and silver mines, rice fields, and in timber, construction and shipping industries—and in houses. These were the survivors from a much larger number captured in Africa, as many died before arriving in the "New World." Scholars call it "the Middle Passage" in English or "Maafa," in Swahili, the "Massive Disaster."

One of the best scholars of the Maafa teaches in the College. Roquinaldo Ferreira, assistant professor of African and African-American history, has combed the archives of Portugal, Brazil, and Angola to produce a fine book entitled Atlantic Microhistory: Slaving, Transnational Networks, and Cross-Cultural Exchange in Angola. It is a fascinating kaleidoscope of the agencies and purposes that propelled the transatlantic trade in slaves, set against the backdrop of the slaves themselves, as well as slave traders, African chiefs, African witches, mulattoes, Portuguese judges, and Brazilian and Portuguese merchants, reminding us that the global slave trade not only helped shape the modern world economy but also cultures and societies across the Atlantic, in the Old and the New Worlds alike.

The second kind of globalism that Ghana helped to usher in was a new kind of political and intellectual thought, through the works of men like Kwame Nkrumah, the first Prime Minister and then President of independent Ghana; and W.E.B. Du Bois, who, at the invitation of Nkrumah, spent the last years of his life in Ghana writing Encyclopedia Africana. Nkrumah was educated at Lincoln University in Pennsylvania in the 1930s, a historically black school, and was conscious about being part of what we have come to call the African-American diaspora. Nkrumah's perspective was instinctively and foremost an internationalist one and, specifically, an "Atlanticist" one—not necessarily in the way the term is used to denote a perspective on Europe and America, but in the larger sense that includes both Americas as well as Africa. Even as he focused on national autonomy and economic independence for Ghana, he thought simultaneously about the need to bring resources together to address the imbalance of resources and life chances in the world system. He advocated Pan-Africanism, contributing to the establishment of the Organization of the African Unity (and later African Union); he was also a pioneer of Third World solidarity in the form of international non-alignment (one of the most stunning buildings in Accra, the capital, is dedicated to the non-aligned movement). That movement had its heyday beginning with the Bandung conference in the mid-1950s and extending to the late 1970s. If it later proved to be something of a chimera, both the non-aligned movement and the African Union proved successful in one of their most important goals: helping stamp out the last vestiges of colonialism and minority rule in Africa. Today one can hardly set foot in Ghana without being reminded of Nkrumah's towering presence and impact.

W.E.B. Du Bois died in Ghana in 1963 at the age of 95, one

day before Martin Luther King Jr.'s March on Washington. In The Souls of the Black Folk, he spoke metaphorically of the pursuit of the Golden Fleece, which he likened to the profits of the cotton industry: "Have you ever seen a cotton-field white with the harvest, its golden fleece hovering above the black earth like a silvery cloud edged with dark green, its bold white signals waving like the foam of billows from Carolina to Texas across that Black and human Sea?" But the Golden Fleece could have been any number of things. It could have meant the gold in search of which the Europeans first came to Ghana, or any profit in search of which the African-American diaspora became the pawn—or for that matter, the very notion of progress, which often seems to have receded in Ghana and many other African countries. I visited DuBois' home in Accra, now a museum, wandered around his study, looked at his ample bookshelves, studied photos of the man—always, the picture of the scholar—and wondered what he would think of the color line in the world today, almost a half-century after his death.

173

Ghana has always been among the wealthiest and socially advanced countries in sub-Saharan Africa, well-endowed with natural resources. It still remains one of the world's top gold producers, and the second largest producer of cocoa. It earns large foreign exchange from timber, diamond, bauxite, manganese, and even electricity from a dam sitting astride the world's largest artificial lake. And it has oil, just discovered off its western coast, near Takoradi. Still, progress remains elusive—both as a notion and as a reality.

Taking a stroll in the labyrinth of the local market in Ta-koradi, I came across yet another kind of globalization, whose specter I had not anticipated. Everywhere I turned in the market were piles and piles of goods to satisfy all the daily needs of ordinary Ghanaians—pots, pans, kettles, plastic ware, shirts, sunglasses, fake watches, shoes, sandals—all made in China. The local goods were only things manufactured by nature: the fruit that falls so abundantly from the trees, the rice grown according to ancient Ghanaian methods (and that slaves brought to the Carolinas), the fish that could be collected through "purse seine" fishing. Everything else seemed to be provided by the factories of China—hardly the kind of global future that Nkrumah would have predicted or hoped for; he dreamed of a self-reliant industrial future for his country. True, there were some manufactured things that were not Chinese. The streets of Takoradi were filled with Nissans, Hyundais, and Volkswagens. But it was also easy to imagine Chinese sedans joining the ranks before long.

W.E.B du Bois wrestled with the idea of the Golden Fleece, understood this time as "progress." He didn't think it was measurable—or for that matter, even recognizable. Is "progress" in the dreams of non-alignment and solidarity, in retrospect so rational, sensible and in fact "progressive"? But it waned as the Cold War alignments themselves disappeared, and as the idea of sustained Third World development succeeded only here and there, not everywhere. Or is it in the ubiquitous Chinese wares, exchanged for the mineral and energy resources excavated from the African soil? And how would we know whether all the progress of today is, as du Bois put it, "the twilight of nightfall or the flush of some faint-dawning day?"

Meanwhile our faculty and students at Semester at Sea sail the world, like Jason and his Argonauts in quest of the Golden Fleece. One would hope that they will have better luck with naming and finding their future.

175

VIRGINIA IN PEKING

LAST WEEK THE COLLEGE opened an office on the campus of Peking University. It is located on the fifth floor of a state-of-the art building, overlooking a stately court-yard, surrounded by stunningly beautiful modern academic buildings that keep springing up, as the Chinese are wont to say, like bamboo shoots after the spring rain. We expect to put this office at Peking University to good use to facilitate research collaboration and faculty and student exchanges between the two universities.

NOVEMBER 2009

At the ceremony for signing the agreement, President Casteen spoke of the growing bond between two great public universities. The parallels between the two places are numerous. The University of Virginia was founded not because Thomas Jefferson wanted another shining beacon of enlightenment and secularism but because he felt the university was a prerequisite for the survival of the Republic and the American Revolution that had given birth to it. The creation of Peking University was also an act of desperate hope, seeking to establish modern learning in order to revive an ailing nation in a world dominated by the Western powers. In both universities academic freedom was to be the guiding principle governing the conduct of all their affairs.

But Peking University has had a more turbulent history. Academic freedom in the best tradition of the German research university (which is essentially what was sought at Peking University) was grafted onto the body of a Chinese tradition where the intellectuals actually laid claim to power. It turned out to be a combustible combination. In traditional China, intellectuals (or the literati) came from local landed gentry and, upon passing the state examination, they became government officials. Thus the intellectuals in China identified with the state, and took a certain responsibility for its welfare. This sense of political agency took new forms at the newly founded Peking University.

Throughout its history Peking University produced intellectuals, leaders, and rebels of every conceivable political stripe, and was responsible for triggering major social and political movements in China. A birthplace of the May Fourth Movement which gave cultural expression to Chinese nationalism, it also spawned Chinese communism by producing a number of founding members of the Chinese Communist Party—even Mao Zedong worked there as a staff librarian. In addition to Communist leaders, it also produced nationalist thinkers on the right and liberal thinkers somewhere in between. Nearly all major historical events involved agitations on its campus, whether be it the Cultural Revolution or the Tiananmen Square protests.

Thomas Jefferson famously said that the University of Virginia will be based on the "illimitable freedom of the human mind." He also followed that "for here, we are not afraid to follow truth where it may lead, nor to tolerate any error so long as reason is left free to combat it."

At Peking University, reason is still not fully free to combat the errors of its complex history. But it is claiming its rightful place as one of Asia's greatest universities, and it is teeming with scholars from all over the world, engaged in all kinds of cutting-edge research. The Chinese government accounts for nearly one quarter of global funding in scientific research—and the beneficiaries are the universities like Peking University, China's flagship in higher education. When I see their science laboratories, my jaw drops, not just because they are state of the art, but also because they are able to build them at a fraction of what they would cost in Charlottesville.

With such vigorous investment in research and scholarship, China is finally returning to its greatness, again putting intellectuals and learning at the center of its civilization.

At the moment of this historical turn, I am full of hope for the future and for greater collaboration between our two great institutions. When students from all over China and around the world walk down the hall of that beautiful building to arrive at a sign that says, "University of Virginia," they may appreciate the truth so eloquently described by Jefferson: "That ideas should freely spread from one to another over the globe, for the moral and mutual instruction of man, and improvement of his condition, seems to have been peculiarly and benevolently designed by nature . . . like fire, expansible over all space, without lessening their density in any point, and like the air in which we breathe, move, and have our physical being, incapable of confinement or exclusive appropriation."

A PASSAGE TO CHINA

HUMEN–MOUTH OF THE TIGER–IS where the Pearl River flows into the South China Sea. This is also where the Confucian commissioner of the Qing court, Lin Zexu, tried to turn back the barbarians—the private merchants importing opium from Britain—by dumping two and a half million pounds of opium into the sea. This story never ceases to animate the Chinese; the driver of the mini-van carrying our small delegation of three from the College, pointed to the sea and shouted, "aa-pin!," Chinese for opium.

The College team was in southern China earlier this month for a "look-see" for a possible scholarly "tripod" that would connect scholars and students from the College, Peking University, and the Hong Kong University of Science and Technology (HKUST). We already have established collaborations at the level of individual scientists in Astronomy, Physics, Environmental Sciences, and Mathematics—but we wanted to explore ways to leverage those relationships to further collaborative research, share labs, and generate joint proposals to the National Science Foundation, both in the U.S. and China. We are also starting to pool our resources for Asian Humanities, where the College is long on aspiration but short on resources. Because English is the lingua franca in Hong Kong, it provides a congenial environment for our students to experience China without interrupting their studies with extensive language training. Now, as it was back in the days of the Opium War, Hong Kong is also a passage to China.

Last year, with the help of HKUST, we opened a small office on the campus of Peking University, not far from the seat of the Chinese mandarinate, old and new. This is the China the pundits have in mind when they speak of hegemonic competition and the clash of civilizations: the China with a long history of control over tributary states, the China that believes today as it has for so many centuries in the moral claim to its leadership (derived from a Confucian rather than Jeffersonian morality), the China that relies on the state to guide the compression of the entire industrial history of the

West into a mere three decades in China.

But it turns out that Hong Kong serves as the passage to more than one China. The other China is in the south. It is the antithesis of the one in the north—maritime, mercantile, practical, and far more open to the world—and yet quickly folding into the tried-and-true developmental design emanating from Peking up north. Our partners, HKUST and Peking University, are establishing branch campuses and otherwise collaborating with research outfits in Shenzhen and Nansha, each about an hour from Hong Kong, with an aim to create a vibrant scientific corridor for southern China, teeming with engineers and researchers from around the world. The Pearl River Delta is not satisfied with being the factory for the world; it wants to be its scientific brain as well. So we were in Humen, at the Mouth of the Tiger, to be present at the creation, watching the future unfold in ways that seemed idiosyncratically Chinese.

Nansha, of which Humen is part, is a sleepy fishing village. Surveying it on a rainy afternoon, one would think modernity stopped at its gate. Outside the ancestral hall for the local "Mok" clan—used in recent decades as everything from the Communist Party district office to a grain warehouse, it had been desecrated during the Cultural Revolution and was recently restored as a place of remembrance for the local Moks—mangy dogs stroll the streets; two women sit in the darkness of a store that has nothing to sell, one silently pulling yarn off an old sweater and another rolling it into a ball, in perfect syncopation; and a toothless man with a leathery face sits in a doorway, repairing an old wool glove that would have ended in the trash heap elsewhere. The only signs of modernity are the flyers on the alley walls, warning migrant workers of the perils of sexually transmitted diseases, and in case they cannot read, with illustrations of how to protect themselves.

Amid this apparent timelessness, the Chinese government is staking a future for southern China. The future comes in concentric circles, with the outer circle forming the scientific corridor that is part of the Guangzhou development strategy; inside the circle, the Nansha Information Technology Park; and at its center, the centerpiece, a graduate research university that will focus on applied genomics, polymer processing, atmospheric research, composite materials technology, bioengineering and its devices, green products and processing technologies—you name it.

183

It was déjà vu all over again: in the 1980s Deng Xiaoping had created the so-called Special Economic Zones that are really prophylactic realms, protected from the constraints and cultures of the rest of the mainland, where a foreign investor could walk in with a suitcase, and have all his or her business needs met, from new hotels and restaurants to manufacturing and exporting the products. The Chinese are taking a page out of that successful strategy, but instead of a one-stop special economic zone, they are offering the world a one-stop science and technology zone, with a research university at its heart. The university facilities are new and shining, and they stand there empty: If you build it, the Chinese government seems to be saying, they will come. But this time "it" is not a baseball field but a high-tech university, and "they" are not old players but new players, the high-tech scientists of the future.

One hundred seventy years ago, William Gladstone, newly elected to Parliament, denounced Britain's Opium War, asking whether there had ever been "a war more unjust in origin, a war more calculated to cover this country with permanent disgrace." Deeper than the disgrace to the British then is the moral indignation that still lives in the heart of the Chinese now, an indignation still capable of turning an ordinary Chinese into a strident nationalist in a heartbeat. In a letter to Queen Victoria that was a litany of grievances against Britain (not unlike our own Declaration of Independence), Commissioner Lin asked where the conscience of Britain had gone. Unlike America, China lost the war. But they won a moral claim against the West that still motivates them, a sense that the future is now theirs, set free by a technological prowess that no longer belongs exclusively to the West.

LEAVING THE COMFORT ZONE

THIS IS THE "FIRST LECTURE," which is a College convention—a dean provides the first lecture to the incoming first-year students. I have titled it "Leaving the Comfort Zone," to state the obvious: you have left the comfort of your homes in Virginia and elsewhere in the U.S., to arrive in a city that in the last two centuries went from a barren piece of rock to being a shining metropolis open to all cultures and peoples; and since 1997 it has managed all that while being part of a country that is ruled by a communist party. This city will present you with mind-boggling complexity—in more ways than one.

A week ago I would not have guessed that I would be arriving in Hong Kong, following in the footsteps, as it were, of Edward Snowden. A 29-year old American with a rapid succession of careers—in the military, the CIA, the National Security Agency and then Booz Allen Hamilton—he is also perched somewhere in this same city. He leaked documents revealing that the United States government has engaged in surveillance of citizens—its own and others—in an effort to thwart terrorist plots. Instantly a debate ensued; it was a familiar debate on the fine line between "privacy" on the one hand, and "national security" on the other. Trying to find a few needles in the tetra-bytes of haystacks, the government was riffling through emails, Facebook, twitters, and phone calls of a multitude of foreign suspects, and the American citizens they might have contacted. The idea was to look for patterns in the communications and store them in case they prove useful in the future.

The new modes of communication arriving in the past fifteen or twenty years provide such instant connection and gratification that we ease into an intellectual comfort zone without much concern. Then someone downloads confidential information, and the notions of "privacy" and "national security" are instantly juxtaposed in adversarial and oppositional ways. We are now forced to question the meaning of privacy in the 21st century, in a digitally interconnected world where citizens give up their privacy unknowingly to the government, but also willingly and effortlessly to commercial entities who trail us through myriad social networks. Our conceptions of individual inviolability and privacy, rooted in eighteenth-century dictums, encounter a world flung open to anonymous servers, humming quietly along and grazing on our every word.

We also search, in this new century and this Brave New World, for a new meaning of the term "national security." The onset of the Cold War in the 1940s wrought dramatic changes akin to those we face today, as the U.S. for the first time developed a permanent standing army, hundreds of military bases abroad, and a new national security state at home. This new world was understandable because security was a matter pitting one nation against another; in many ways it merely brought the U.S. into the great power milieu that Europe had known for centuries. The primary adversary was also a modern state, the Soviet Union; the U.S. and the Soviet Union offered two alternative, top-to-bottom models of what modernity meant.

Now our enemies are not other states, but inchoate, invisible, implacable foes who seem to abhor everything we stand for, and who fight by means fair and foul. By these standards, the zone of Cold War rivalry was comfortable, at least in its boundaries. The threat of communism stimulated a vast expansion of the American state and its intelligence apparatus, dealing with existential threats abroad. But now the apparatus doesn't know where to look: the quarry might be an Arab-American citizen in Yemen or a college kid wearing a backpack on his way to the Boston Marathon. So in a world where everyone can be both target and targeter, no one can escape. We need somehow to leave the comfort zone of Cold War and par-for-the-course national security dilemmas, rethink our assumptions, and start an important debate on the meaning of the national security state in our time, a very different and unprecedented era. That is the responsibility of the democratic citizenry, which is after all the purpose of the liberal arts education.

From his hideout in Hong Kong, Mr. Snowden also leveled charges against the United States government for hacking into government, business, and university computers in China, when our news media had it the other way around—one article after another about China's assault on our cyber-system. The question has become whether Snowden is a concerned citizen and patriot speaking truth to power, and in so doing disclosing a new surveillance campaign in American history, or a traitor aiding and abetting another sovereign government. And if the international system is no longer a system of nations acting as separate agents, but a shadowy world of clandestine digital break-ins by public and private entities, one might ask what is left of the meaning of nationalism and patriotism.

So, you and I seem to have left our comfort zones by arriving in this city, just as a new world drama crashes on our familiar shores and unfolds before our very eyes. I do hope that you will pay very close attention to the events of the last couple of weeks, and continue to do so even after Mr. Snowden departs Hong Kong, as he likely will. This is not a comfortable discussion but a necessary one; from it you will learn a great deal about relations between our government and China, and between China and Hong Kong; and you will learn a lot about their legal systems.

"Leaving the comfort zone" is the essential means that we deploy in seeking truth, which is the aim of our education—our liberal arts education. For all the ink spilled to define the purpose of a liberal arts education—and there is an ocean of it—nothing is so fundamental and important as our quest to understand the truth about ourselves, our circumstances, and our predicaments. Inside the comfort zone, that truth is impossible to obtain. To cite the venerable metaphor of Plato's cave, you can see the shadow on the wall, but cannot discern the truth of the shadow without stepping out of the cave and into the light.

I envy you for having a great summer curriculum. Many of you are taking a course on Max Weber, jointly taught by Professors Krishan Kumar of UVA and Joshua Derman of HKUST. Max Weber pioneered something called comparative sociology. His core idea was stunningly simple; cognition is not possible except through comparison—you know what is, by knowing what is not. Weber claimed that there was a profound relationship between a particular kind of culture and religion, and the rise of capitalism. To establish a truth that could withstand scrutiny, he had to study the major religions of the world, to argue why Protestantism and its work ethic was conducive to material accumulation under capitalism—but not Catholicism, not Islam, not Hinduism, and not Confucianism. He stepped out of the Prussian intellectual milieu, his comfort zone, to read the best scholarship on the religions of the world.

You will be reading his "Religion of China." An Occidentalist to the core, Weber found it difficult to assign rationality to the world outside of the European tradition, and his "Religion of China" is, in my view, a deeply flawed account of Chinese culture—as flawed as the best writings on China in the late nineteenth century, which is to say, very flawed. But there are brilliant passages in this book, transcending passages of comparative sociology. And even when he was wrong, Max Weber had more interesting ideas in his little finger than many of the sociologists in the decades that followed. I hope so much that you will delight in all his ideas, interesting when he was wrong as when he was right. Regardless, you will appreciate the effort he took to discover and express truth according to his own lights.

You will be taking "A New History of China, 1700-2000" by Professor James Lee, one of the greatest historical and economic sociologists of China. In that course you will explore an entirely different way to perceive global history, a quantitative route to making explicit comparisons between China

190

and the West. Rather than recast the trajectories of modernity through ideal types as Weber did—some composite pictures of the "west" versus the "rest"—you will learn to anchor your analysis on hard data to the extent that we can excavate them: living standards and human development as measured by consumption, life expectancy, and literacy (which in China were roughly comparable to the West until the mid-19th century). Looking at modern history through the Chinese prism—community, ethnicity, family, freedom, gender, life, power, property, religion, rights, rules, sexuality—one begins to accumulate more evidence, allowing us to think more fully and maturely about how societies evolve and are structured. We shed light where we once looked through the glass darkly. In other words the study of modern China should help us better understand our society and ourselves.

The professors at Virginia and HKUST have also come together to offer courses on the environment, to provide historical perspectives on pollution control, water quality, and food security. I know you will explore firsthand the wild life refuge between Shenzhen and Hong Kong, and marine fish culture management zones.

In another one of your classes, you will develop tools for thinking about complex technological systems as they adapt to change. You will think deeply and carefully about the implications of the rise of megacities: energy and water systems, natural resource availability, transportation, health and population—and how they all relate to climate change.

In the next twelve years, China plans to move 250 million people living in rural areas to cities; our classes will provide ways for you to understand the transformation of this great mass of peasants into urban citizens.

In closing, allow me to recount in one more way the virtue of leaving your comfort zones. You are the first generation of the Americans whose lives will be affected in so many important ways by the country where you stand today: China. It may not seem so now, but the peace and prosperity of the United States depends very much on understanding China. In no small measure the effective collaboration between the two countries—or their effective estrangement—will determine whether we will have a peaceful twenty-first century, one of cooperation in a US-Chinese condominium; or a falling away from each other into a perilous future. I sincerely hope that the inaugural class of the Jefferson Global Seminars will be agents of peace and collaboration, as you must.

A DIFFERENT KIND OF DIVERSITY

IT WAS NOT UNTIL the 1950s that the first African-American students graduated from the College; the first class of women graduated in 1974, thirty-five years ago. Diversity seemed a little more elusive for us than for other distinguished universities—until today. When you step into Newcomb Hall, along with the clanking of the utensils, you hear Spanish, Filipino, Korean, and Chinese.

Last week I was in Singapore, attending an event organized by Gordon Kirtland (College '77; Darden '81) and Chew

Mee Foo Kirtland (Darden '81) of Singapore. They are stalwart supporters of the College, pillars of the local U.Va. community, and parents of a rising second-year student. Even under the threat of a tropical rainstorm, the die-hard Wahoos of Singapore showed up at the event—some forty-five alumni, parents and students, wearing orange and blue. Those were the only colors they had in common; it was the most diverse group of 'Hoos I have had the honor to meet in my first year as Dean.

There they were: The Peranakans (the descendents of Chinese immigrants who came to Singapore in the eighteenth century), Tamils, Punjabis, Malays, and Thais who reside permanently in the city state, and sojourners from everywhere in the United States, working in the financial sector for UBS, Morgan Stanley, and Standard Chartered Bank. Together, they were Exhibit A of what has made one of the most improbable of the twentieth century's fairy tales come true, when a colonial entrepôt turned into one of the world's greatest financial centers. Singapore has parlayed this terrific diversity of humanity—open, munificent, and welcoming—into a vital asset for the future.

Twenty years ago, the government of Singapore presented the world with a political philosophy called, "Asian values." It was mocked in some quarters as the antithesis of the self-evident truths and transcendent values we hold dear in the West. But buried in the din of criticism was the truth that "Asia" for Singapore is a very diverse and contentious community, making "Asian values" something almost universal. The qualities that have made Singapore successful are the qualities of maritime commerce, which turn out to be the qualities of a great university: open, multinational, multilingual, multicultural.

In my meeting with the Singaporean Wahoos, I shared the news that the College now offers language instruction in a number of Asian languages, including Chinese, Japanese, Korean, Hindi, Urdu and soon, Bengali—and hopes in time to be recognized by the Department of Education as a National Resource Center for both East Asia and South Asia. This news was received with great delight—but at the same time, they know, as I do, that the College is a deeply multicultural place. And as our Singapore alumni demonstrate so proudly, it has been for longer than people realize.

THE UNIVERSITY AND INDUSTRIAL POLICY

SITTING DOWN FOR DINNER at an Italian restaurant in Seoul on the last day of my trip through East Asia, I noticed a long table with a dozen reporters huddled around it. Presiding was an old friend of mine, currently serving as Dean of the Engineering School at Seoul National University, the top university in Korea. From the way the reporters were intently jotting down his remarks, you would think the dean was a major public figure, not just another academic running a school. Between morsels of pasta I eavesdropped on the conversation between the dean and journalists, picking up terms like "competitiveness," "US News & World Report," "measurable progress," and of course, "benchmarks"—the vocabulary of excellence and competition, the lingua franca of higher education these days.

Curious at the preponderance of reporters at the dinner table, I asked if any of them covered Seoul National University exclusively. They laughed and said that they all did. In fact, there are some twenty reporters who cover this single university—as if it were the White House, or in the Korean context, the Blue House. The size of the press corps assigned to Seoul National University should erase any doubt in anyone's mind about the central role universities are playing in the carefully plotted future of that country—and through a well-known Korean mechanism that dares not speak its name: industrial policy. Seoul National University made it to the top 50 universities in the world in the US News & World Report rankings —something that would have been unthinkable only a few years ago—because of the large flow of R&D support provided by the government.

The situation is not dissimilar at the National University of Singapore (NUS) and Hong Kong University of Science and Technology (HKUST), the two universities I visited on this same trip, and with whom the College is cautiously exploring programmatic possibilities. These universities are deeply cherished by their governments, as if they are national treasures—and not just because education, along with the institutions of family and the state, have formed the pillars of the Chinese civilization. Today higher education in Hong Kong and Singapore is the engine of massive social transformation, turning yesterday's beehive of manufacturing into tomorrow's global hub of knowledge and knowledge-intensive industries. Even in laissez faire Hong Kong and Singapore, the university has become the agent of industrial policy.

Not surprisingly, the governments of Singapore and Hong Kong are approaching this the only way they know how—by drawing in the greatest talents from around the world, and making alliances with the best and the brightest in North America, Europe, and Asia. The moment that they understood that universities accelerate economic growth, they went at it with vengeance. Determined to make their once sleepy universities into some of the very best in the world, they connected them to the rest of the world, and with amazing speed.

Singapore and Hong Kong are impatient cities. Even before they knew how to manufacture, they drew in foreign investments; even before they sold at home, they sold abroad. Now, even before their universities develop their own talent, they are drawing talent from abroad; their campuses teem with Nobel laureates and US national academy members giving lectures, running conferences, and in general transiting in and out. They have Memoranda of Understanding with world-famous universities—for student exchanges, branch campuses, joint-degree programs—anything to quicken the circulation of knowledge. This kind of international traffic invigorates scholarship, but it also generates reputations, reputations that are reflected in rankings.

On my way out to the airport the next morning in driving rain, I got a call from one of the reporters at the dinner. He wanted to know what I thought about the quality of the Korean universities (which I said was excellent), and whether some of their best colleges might have the College of Arts and Sciences at Virginia as benchmark (a worthy goal, I said). The great universities in Asia and the University of Virginia all have the same aspiration: to provide our students with the skills necessary to learn the truth, however it might be defined. The truth, after all, is what Aristotle said was the point of education. But the philosopher also said there was a another point to education: to inculcate virtue.

And there's the rub: how do you rank virtue?

199